Protecting His Workmanship

teaching your child God's design for sexual purity

Jeff and Pam Koehlinger

"For we are God's workmanship, created in Christ Jesus to do good works, which God prepared in advance for us to do."

Ephesians 2:10

Protecting His Workmanship

teaching your child God's design for sexual purity

First Printing: October 2004
Library of Congress Control Number: 2004109664
ISBN: 0-9715911-4-8

All Bible verses are from the NIV unless otherwise noted

Acknowledgements

We thank God for the gift of our sons, Andrew and Ryan, for whom our passion for purity was first ignited. Our deep love for them and the sobering conviction that we are stewards of God in discipling them to imitate Christ in all areas of their lives for God's purposes and glory were the inspiration behind the family exercises that became this book. Andrew, Ryan, and the family we have become are truly a testimony to the power of God to bring about His workmanship in our lives despite our imperfect efforts as parents. We pray that God will continue that work in your lives and empower you to pursue lives of purity and full obedience to His will.

We thank God for our own parents, who taught us from an early age that we were created in the image of God and that our bodies and hearts belong to Him. We did not honor their instruction perfectly, but we would not be who we are today without it.

We wish to thank Bruce Malone, founder of Search for the Truth Publications, and Darryl White, executive director of our local Pregnancy Resource Center, friends who saw potential in the initial versions of our family studies, approached us with the idea of publishing this book, and encouraged and supported us throughout the publication process. They have been selfless and patient instruments of God in showing us the urgent need for this kind of parent-child workbook and in raising the financial support necessary to make it a reality. We also wish to thank Kathy Stephenson for the many hours she spent in designing the cover and other graphics for the book.

We wish to thank those who edited these studies and worked through earlier versions of them with their own children while this book was being prepared. In particular, we are grateful to Pastors Jay Childs and Mike Mercer (for their theological review and input); Karen Forrester, for proofing the final copy; and Joe Lehman, a treasured brother in Christ, for his editorial suggestions and incredible insight and perspective as a father seeking to deliberately raise his own children in the training and instruction of the Lord. These studies are significantly improved because of their efforts.

We thank God for every single one of the brothers and sisters in Christ who donated the funds for the first publication of this book. Their interest in, enthusiasm for, and financial commitment to this project are a wonderful confirmation that its publication was God's will in God's timing. It has been a humbling privilege to partner with them in this work.

Most of all, we praise God, the Giver of all good gifts, for the opportunity to be used of Him in protecting His workmanship in the next generation. His design of the human body and spirit, His clear instruction in Scripture, and the models of purity He has protected in every generation of a fallen world testify to His unfailing love for us and the beauty of His holiness. May He use these studies for His purposes and be glorified in the life of every parent and every teen He leads to this book.

About the Authors

Jeff and Pam Koehlinger live in Midland, Michigan with their sons, Andrew and Ryan. Jeff is a corporate human resources attorney, and Pam is a stay-at-home wife and mother and occasional free-lance writer. Married for sixteen years, they share a passion for biblical parenting and the unique challenges faced by parents desiring to raise godly children in an increasingly godless culture. Jeff has a particular interest in encouraging and equipping fathers to train their sons in biblical manhood through study, prayer, mentoring, adventure, and rites of passage. As a family, the Koehlingers enjoy biking, water sports, reading aloud, and listening to *Adventures in Odyssey* on long car trips.

Table of Contents

Publisher's Prologue

There are few subjects which parents approach with more fear and trepidation than introducing their children to the awe, beauty, and purpose of human sexuality. Christian parents are too often guilty of avoiding the subject altogether. Yet our sexuality is as much a part of our lives as our spirituality. ***Protecting God's Workmanship*** is one family's efforts to teach their children Godly principles of sexual purity.

Both the authors and publisher have donated 100% of the proceeds from this printing to abstinence training and pregnancy resource center ministries. Consider purchasing additional copies for friends, other families in your church, and relatives in your extended family. They and their children will be blessed by your kindness.

Search for the Truth Publications exists to shine the light of truth on those areas where God's Word is being twisted or ignored. Jesus commanded us to, *"Love the Lord your God with all your heart and with all your soul and with all your mind."* (Matthew 22:37) The great deceiver has intellectually misled millions by undermining their trust in the Bible, using the deception of evolution and the fallacy that there have been billions of years of earth history. He physically destroys tens of millions each year through abortion, sexually transmitted diseases, and euthanasia. The enemy of our souls seeks to destroy us morally with the temptation of sin, especially sexual sin and perversion. Furthermore, Satan has weakened the faith of hundreds of millions of people with the lie of "safe sex" outside of marriage.

This book, and the resources described throughout the book, will help you and your children win the battle which is raging for their hearts, their souls, and their minds.

For His Glory, Share the Truth!

Bruce Malone, Search for the Truth Ministries

Introduction

This project began as a work of love, created by a father for his son. As authors, we pray that it will continue to be a work of love for all those desiring a contemporary, biblical tool with which to begin (or continue) revealing to their teen or pre-teen the beauty, mystery, and wonder of God's design and purposes for marriage and sexual intimacy. This includes Christian families, youth workers and mentors, pregnancy resource centers, and even those who do not yet know Christ, but who could discover His love and holiness in these pages.

When our eldest son, Andrew, demonstrated readiness for specific information and guidance on the important subject of sexual intimacy and marriage, we began looking for holistic, biblical resources on this topic designed specifically for Christian parents and teens. We wanted to address the physical, emotional, and spiritual aspects of sexual intimacy and how to view all its facets from a biblical perspective. The proper instruction of our children in this area was of particular concern to us because we were keenly aware of the unbiblical messages assaulting our children from every direction in our sex-saturated, relativistic, post-modern society.

As parents, we want our children to take personal ownership of biblical values not just because this is what we have taught them, but because their own study of God's Word convinces them that His design for human sexuality is truly best. As our first son reached adolescence, we wanted to build into him a deep conviction of the importance of sexual purity in singleness and sexual faithfulness in marriage so that he would be well-equipped to live out the truths of God's Word in today's contrary culture. To do this, we needed a resource founded solidly on Scripture which would facilitate both family discussion and personal study by our teen.

We also wanted to share information on sex in a way that would set a pattern for regular, continuing interaction with our children as they grow and develop through their teen years. Ideally, you will have been leading your child to a biblical understanding of sex and marriage in everyday life from early childhood. The earlier you lay the foundation for the explicit discussion of these topics in adolescence, the easier it will be for your teen to internalize God's perspective on these topics instead of the world's.

If your relationship with your teen is weak or strained, now is the time to seek healing and restoration. The time you have left with him in your home is quickly disappearing. And his willingness to listen to and accept your instruction will likely only be in proportion to the strength of your relationship.

Children are not ready the moment they first reach puberty (and certainly not as early as modern educators desire) for all the information they will eventually need to learn about sex. Sex education, like most things, should be progressive, based on the individual child's circumstances, intellectual capacity, exposure to outside influences, individual level of curiosity, and most importantly, spiritual maturity. But when they are ready, their instruction should come from the Bible, not the world.

In this study, we only scratch the surface of many areas. In the months and years to come, you will want to come back to these topics and go deeper with your teen as you develop a strategy together for applying God's command of purity and holiness in your child's life. Such a strategy will serve our children well both while they are young and single, and when they are married.

Because we could not find a resource which fulfilled these objectives in a readily useable format, we put together our own study, intending to use it immediately with Andrew and in the future with our second child, Ryan. However, through a chain of subsequent relationships and events clearly brought about by God, He called us to modify the materials for use by all who share our heart for revealing the beauty of God's plan for sexual intimacy and marriage to young people of both sexes.

Ideally, children should learn the truth about issues as important as those underlying and surrounding sexuality from their parents, but there are many circumstances in our world today in which that is not possible. We hope that this guide will aid adults in various circumstances to reach the teens in their sphere of influence with the truths of God's Word. We believe that in today's world, the Church has been called to preserve a remnant who will remain faithful to God's design for marriage and sexual love. So armed, our teens will be prepared to reveal God's truth to a society which has fallen prey to Satan's lies about sex and love, working to redeem our sex-saturated culture for Christ and to bring God the glory due His name.

Format

This book is divided into six sections. Each section respresents a 1-2 hour session with your child as you discuss a different aspect of God's design for sexual intimacy in their lives. Each session is, in turn, divided into four individual parts.

Part A: The first part is the **Parent Discussion Guide**. Read this section prior to discussing the material with your child. Customize it to fit your style, personal convictions, and comfort level. As you plan each session, leave plenty of time for questions and discussion of the material with your child.

Part B: The **Student Discussion Notes** contains a parallel fill-in-the-blank section for your child to use while you are discussing the material with him. You will notice that the entire book is perforated for easy page removal. Remove the child's pages so that he can fill in the answers while you are discussing the material together. Your teen is much more likely to remember the material if he writes it down while it is being discussed. At the start of each session you may want to staple the pages from parts B & C together and/or put student pages in a binder so they are less likely to become lost.

Part C: The **Student Follow-Up Study** is also to be removed and given to your child after you are done with the intial discussion. This will help her take ownership of the information she has learned and give her an opportunity for personal application and reflection on what she has learned while studying for herself some of what the Bible has to say about each subject.

Part D: The last part of each session is the **Parent Follow-Up Discussion Guide**. It contains suggested answers to the student follow up study. Read this material before having a final discussion of the follow-up study with your child.

This book is not intended to be handed to your child to do independently, but to serve as a vehicle to open the lines of communication as you together discuss God's purpose and design for sexual intimacy in our lives. Each lesson is preceded by an introduction which contains a general summary of that session, hints for making that study more effective, any necessary cautions, and a list of additional resources for parents.

Overview and Approach

These outlines and studies may be used as-is for your family to complete. (You may want to photocopy the student workbook pages, which are found in section B & C of each session, if you intend to use the same workbook for other children in the future). Or you may tailor the outlines and studies as you determine best for your family. We encourage you to change one or all the lessons to match your personal convictions, the needs and maturity level of your child, and the pace at which you desire to disseminate information in your family. Although for simplicity's sake we use the terms "parent(s)" and "son(s)" or "daughter(s)" throughout the workbook, other adults are welcome to adapt the studies for use with clients, mentees, and discipleship groups.

We include the text of most Bible references in the Parent Discussion Guide. Exceptions are passages which are too long to make quoting the entire text feasible in our workbook format. We use the New International Version, but you may wish to use a different version (perhaps one that your teen finds particularly readable).

We cannot tell you *when* to begin this study with your particular child or group. You must determine for yourself, through prayer and close attention to the physical, social, and spiritual development of each child, at what age he is ready for this study. We do not believe that sooner is always better than later for detailed instruction, but we do believe it is best for children to learn the truth from their parents before they are exposed to lies and half-truths from their peers, music, T.V., movies, and other secular influences. Because girls often mature faster than boys and commonly begin to take notice of the opposite sex sooner, you may decide to begin the study with your daughter(s) at an earlier age than you begin it with your son(s). *You know your child best*. We encourage you to protect his or her innocence as long as possible; then, seeking the leading of the Spirit, introduce the subject of sexuality with discretion, honesty, and enthusiasm. If you desire to conduct this study with a child who is not your own son or daughter, we strongly recommend that you consult the child's parent(s) or guardian(s) before you begin.

Tips for a More Effective Study

✓ We encourage you to conduct this study with your child as a couple, rather than assigning the duty/privilege to one parent (most commonly the one who is the same sex as the child). God gave our children two parents – one male and one female – for a reason. Not only should your child have the freedom to come to either of you for counsel and a listening ear, but each of you has something valuable to offer him through your unique experience as a man or a woman. The perspective of the opposite sex is critical to a full and accurate understanding of sex, love, and purity. If you are single parent you will conduct this study alone. Ask God to bring other models and mentors of the opposite sex into your child's life.

✓ Begin by praying as a couple several weeks or months in advance. In addition to the burdens God has laid on your heart for your particular child, you need to:

- Pray for wisdom, transparency, and discretion for you as parents – and for an open and responsive heart for your son or daughter.
- Pray for protection from the enemy as you approach this delicate subject and for consistency as you make these sessions a family priority over the next few weeks.

✓ Invite your child to the study a couple of weeks ahead of time through a letter or other special invitation.

- Tell her that you are excited about conducting this study together and explain why you believe the topic of sexuality is very important to her development as a child of God.
- Ask him to begin thinking about and writing down questions he has about sex, love, singleness, and marriage.
- Build anticipation for the study before it begins by commenting about how much you are looking forward to it and emphasizing that this will be a special, private time for just your child and you.
- We have included a copy of our letter of invitation to our son in Appendix I as an example.

✓ Schedule the six sessions on a regular recurring basis, preferably no less than one week and no more than two weeks apart.

- Schedule a block of time that will allow you and your child to focus without interruption. Home is better than a restaurant, particularly because of the nature of the topics being discussed.
  - Take the phone off the hook.
  - If you have younger children, it would be wise to put them to bed before you begin.
- Allow between one and two hours for each study. The amount of time you need to spend will vary based on the lesson, your teaching style, and the inquisitiveness of your child.

- Consider serving some sort of special refreshment with each session. This creates a relaxed atmosphere and helps set apart this time as something special.

✓ Personalize each study: Add examples from your own life (without disclosing information that should be kept only between husband and wife).
- Our kids need to know that we struggled with many of the same issues they are facing and that, as a result, we have both empathy and wisdom to share.
- If appropriate, share consequences you suffered as a result of disobedience.
- Share specific blessings you have experienced as a result of obedience.

✓ Encourage discussion and dialogue with your child and be prepared with additional follow-up questions if the first question on the outline doesn't provide the desired level of discussion or response.
- Remember that, in addition to giving information and instruction to your child, these studies are designed to give you a window into her heart and mind.
- Whenever possible, use questions that require explanation or discussion, rather than a simple "yes" or "no" answer. If nothing else, regularly ask your child *why* he answered a question that way.
- Reassure your child before and during each session that you want to pursue a frank and regular dialogue about all aspects of life, even areas like sex, that are sometimes sensitive or awkward.

✓ Begin and end each session with prayer.
- In our home, Dad prayed to begin each session, while Dad, Mom, and our son ended each session by praying together.
- Strongly encourage your child to pray out loud during these times. By doing so he will begin to internalize what he has learned and to depend on God for putting what he has learned into practice before he even walks away from each session.

✓ Open the Bible. We do not include the entire scriptural text in the Student Discussion Notes in order to encourage students to open their Bibles and read what God has to say directly from His Word.

✓ Begin each session (except the first) with a review of the Follow-Up Study from the prior lesson, being sure to give special attention to the last question of each follow-up lesson, which asks if the student has any questions from the prior session. If you regularly receive a "no questions" response, dig a bit deeper and gently try to open the window into your child's heart a little wider.

✓ Encourage questions and discussion during the time between lessons as your child works through the Follow-Up Study and processes what you studied during your time together. Car rides with one or both parents and the teen are ideal opportunities to bring up these topics and to encourage discussion. (Boys, in particular, often find it difficult to talk while face-to-face. They frequently prefer to talk while working or playing with you side-by-side.)

✓ Require memorization of a least one (if not all) of the Scripture references at the end of each Follow-Up Study. The Bible is very clear on the important role that memorizing and meditating on Scripture plays in impressing biblical truths on our hearts and empowering us to live in obedience to God. (Psalm 119:11, 105)

General Precautions

✓ As we have already emphasized, you must personalize this study for the needs of your family. Use discernment in what you choose to share with your child, and make sure everything is age-appropriate.

✓ Review each lesson ahead of time to ensure consistency with your theology and personal convictions. We believe some aspects of the topics we discuss are non-negotiable (based on biblical law or principle – e.g. sex is permissible only between one man and one woman and only in marriage). We also believe that some other aspects are more open to interpretation and individual conscience (areas of Christian liberty – e.g. teen dating). Although you may wish to discuss other perspectives, you should, of course, teach what you believe is best for your child.

✓ You do not have to answer every question your child may have on these topics at this time. You may decide that your child is not yet ready for some information. Handle this with sensitivity: Explain to your child that you desire to be open and honest with him and that, at the appropriate time, you will give him the information for which he has asked, but that right now he needs to trust you to protect him by keeping this information temporarily "on hold."

✓ Be especially vigilant in your marriage relationship during this study. Expect and plan for obstacles and tempation. Satan does not want us teaching these truths to our children and will do whatever is in his power to prevent the study from taking place or to diminish its effectiveness with our children. His strategy may include attacking your marriage relationship, particularly through sexual temptation or stagnancy with your spouse. Make it a top priority to spend time together as a couple each week and to be purposeful about fostering intimacy between the two of you. Enlist the support of several close friends who will regularly pray for you and your marriage during this critical period.

Encouragement

✓ Initially, discussing the topics introduced in this study will probably be as uncomfortable for your child as it is for you. But we want to encourage you, from personal experience, that it will get easier! We were surprised at how well the first session went once we got going. If you are relaxed and open, your son or daughter will pick up on your attitude and feel more at ease too.

✓ Our children need and want us to have these kinds of discussions with them. While they may not show it, they will appreciate, and may even look forward to, these study sessions!

✓ God will bless your faithfulness. He knows our inadequacy for the task and delights in making up for our insufficiencies. Our part as parents is to plan and follow through on training, using God's Word as our instruction manual. God's part is to work through us to impart wisdom to our children and to redeem our culture, one obedient teen at a time.

We are excited that you have decided to take this journey with us! Your faithfulness in seeking out this resource, setting aside time to prepare and go through the lessons with your family, and following up with further discussions appropriate to your child's growing maturity will be rewarded by God. We can accomplish nothing on our own, but He promises to demonstrate His strength in our weakness (2 Cor. 12:9). Our heavenly Father has appointed us to train up our children in the way they should go (Proverbs 22:6), to come alongside them and impress His truth upon them (Deuteronomy 6:6-7), to plant and nurture the seeds and trust Him for the fruit (1 Corinthians 3:6). May God bless, above and beyond all that you ask or imagine, your children's obedience to His call to holiness!

Session 1:

Physical Changes and Sexual Love – The Nuts and Bolts

Session Purpose and Themes

Session Summary:

This session will be the traditional "birds & bees" talk, including an introduction to some of the sexual and anatomical terms your teen may need defined. The discussion will also focus on the changes teens are or will be experiencing in their own bodies, how the way we dress affects the opposite sex, and the influence that books, magazines, and movies can have on our perception of love, sex, and marriage.

Session Themes:

- Adolescence is a period of intense growth in all areas (spiritual, social, emotional, and physical). It is important for teens to know and understand the types of changes they will go through and to remember that each person will experience those changes in the special and unique timing God has in store for him. (Psalm 139:13-14)
- One area of physical change is in the unique development of the male and female anatomies. This is a natural process that is part of our preparation for responsibly enjoying the gift of sexual love that God has given to men and women.
- Sexual love is a beautiful thing designed by God for a husband and a wife to enjoy only within the bounds of a lifelong marriage relationship. It is a physically and emotionally intense expression of love between a man and a woman, in addition to being God's way of bringing new children into the world in a context that best meets their needs.

Hints for a More Effective Study

- If you feel awkward as you approach the first session, acknowledge as much to your teen. Remind her that this awkwardness is due to our fallen condition. (See Genesis 2:25; 3:10-11.) Likely your son or daughter is also uncomfortable and will feel more at ease just knowing you feel the same way. Assure your teen (and yourself) that it will get easier as you go along and that the benefits of a candid discussion of these issues far outweigh any initial feelings of uneasiness.
- Emphasize various aspects of the session differently, particularly the mechanics of sex and reproduction, depending on whether your teen is a boy or a girl.
- You may wish to use the anatomical diagrams located in Appendix II to help you explain the various parts of the male and female anatomies and the mechanics of sexual love.
- When you discuss the mechanics of sexual love, we suggest beginning by asking your teen to explain what he thinks he already knows. This will help you assess the amount of detail you need to provide and any misconceptions which may already exist and need to be corrected.

Precautions

- **Define Standards**
Much of the first half of this session will raise questions about the types of clothes, books, movies, and music that are appropriate for young Christian men and women. You should spend time as a couple, if you haven't already, defining the standards you wish to establish for your family in these areas. As you do so, make sure you are careful to distinguish between what is explicit in Scripture, what is your interpretation of scriptural principles, and what is merely your own personal taste and preference. This will help you avoid "exasperating" your child (Eph. 6:4) by falsely implying that your personal standards are all explicitly rooted in biblical law. Focus on helping your teen understand both the **moral** and the **practical** reasons for the standards you have set for your family in all these areas.

- **Plan Age-Appropriate Terminology**
If your child is young and/or less mature and you do not wish to explore all the anatomical and sexual terms covered in this session, simply skip over those details in the Parent's Discussion Guide. Your student does not have these words already printed in his Student Discussion Notes; he has blank spaces in which to take whatever notes you wish to give him.

- **Take Your Time**
It might be tempting to rush through the anatomical and sexual sections of this session, simply because these topics may be awkward for both you and your child to discuss. It is important, though, that you take your time on these topics – in part because they can be confusing when introduced for the first time, in part because the information your child has already gained from other sources is likely to be wrong, and in part because taking time to talk about these things now will help both you and your teen begin to feel more comfortable talking about them in the future. Establishing open, comfortable lines of communication in this area is an important goal of this entire six-part study.

Additional Resources

Arthur, Kay. *Sex . . . According to God: How to Walk with Purity in a World of Temptation*. Colorado Springs: Waterbrook Press, 2003.

Dobson, James. *Preparing for Adolescence: How to Survive the Coming Years of Change*. Ventura, California: Gospel Light Publications, 1999. This tool comes in various forms: family tape or CD pack, family guide and workbook, workbook for youth ages 9 to 14, and group guide for use by churches. It centers on 20 ten-minute sessions of activities and discussion starters to facilitate parents and kids talking together about important issues, including sexuality.

Gresh, Dannah. *Secret Keeper: The Delicate Power of Modesty*. Chicago: Moody Publishers, 2002.

Weidman, Jim & Janet. Ledbetter, J. Ottis & Gail. *Spiritual Milestones: A Guide to Celebrating Your Children's Spiritual Passages*. Colorado Springs: Cook Communications, 2001. Questions 1 & 2 in the Student Follow-up Study are adapted from this book (pp. 53-54).

Part 1A - Parent Discussion Guide

***Introductory comments*:**

- As you grow toward adulthood, you will experience (or have already begun to experience) a dramatic series of physical and emotional changes. One such change is in the area of sexuality.
- In this session, we will explore the most significant physical, emotional, and social changes you are going to experience in the next few years, and we will talk candidly with you about the "nuts and bolts" of sexual love (what it is and how it works).
- We know this may feel awkward at first, but we want you to be free and open with us about your thoughts, feelings, and questions. In return, we will be as candid and honest with you as we can. We want to become comfortable talking with you about things like love, sex, and marriage, both in structured discussions like this and in regular conversation over the coming years.
- Ask whatever questions you have. We will answer your questions as directly as we can, and in a way that is appropriate for your age. If there is information for which we believe you are not yet ready, we will tell you that and ask you to trust us to tell you what you need to know when the time is right.

Note to parents: Try to recall any "birds and bees" talks you had with your own parents. If you had talks like this with your parents, consider sharing how awkward you felt but how grateful you are that your parents took the time to explain things you needed and wanted to know but may have been hesitant to bring up yourself. If you did not have a talk like this, share what you feel you missed and how you want something better for your teen. Add any other comments you want to share as you begin.

I. Adolescence: A Period of Growth and Change in All Areas

- Read Luke 2:52 and emphasize how this verse reveals that Jesus grew physically, spiritually, and socially.

  As you enter the teen years, you are growing and maturing just as Jesus did:
  - ❖ Physically (height, strength, hormonal balance, etc.)
  - ❖ Spiritually (Bible studies, corporate and personal worship, family devotions, personal quiet times, Sunday school class, etc.)
  - ❖ Socially (school, youth group, sports, camps and retreats, etc.)
  - ❖ Intellectually (school, clubs, etc.)

A. Changes During Adolescence

Note to parents: Answers to the following two questions will vary depending on the gender, age, physical development, and maturity level of your child.

What kinds of physical, social, or emotional changes are you currently experiencing?
What kinds of physical, social, or emotional changes can you expect to experience in the next few months and years?

Both Boys & Girls:

- Increasing height
- Hormonal changes, which cause many of the effects listed below
- Oily skin and acne
- Hair growth all over the body, including facial hair for boys
- Mood swings
- New interests, activities, and friends (and the loss of others)
- Increased interest in and attraction to the opposite sex
- "Childishness" (Pro. 29:15) and "foolishness" (Pro. 22:15) changing to maturity (1Cor. 13:11)
- Increasing adult privileges and responsibilities

Boys:

- Voice change
- Enlargement of testicles and penis
- Physical (erection) and mental (sexual thoughts) responses to visual stimuli
- Nocturnal emissions, also known as "wet dreams" (*Note to parents*: Emphasize that this is a natural way for the body to rid itself of extra semen; it is not a bodily function which a man can control. He should not be ashamed when this happens because it is neither wrong nor immoral.)
- Weight gain and increasing muscle mass

Girls:

- Development of breasts and hips
- Menstruation/ovulation
- Ability to become pregnant
- A desire to be noticed by boys and a physical impulse to be "close" and affectionate with a boy.

Note to parents: Discuss differences between boys and girls and their strongest temptations. For example, girls this age typically do not feel significant sexual arousal, as much as the desire to receive male attention through physical "play" and cuddling. Train your child to be sensitive to the vulnerabilities of the other sex and to guard against her own areas of greatest temptation.

B. Timing of Adolescence

❖ Your own physical changes will occur in the special timing that God has designed just for you. (Psalm 139:13-16)

- Read Psalm 139:13-16 – "For You created my inmost being; you knit me together in my mother's womb. I praise You because I am fearfully and wonderfully made; your works are wonderful, I know that full well. My frame was not hidden from You when I was made in the secret place. When I was woven together in the depths of the earth, Your eyes saw my unformed body. All the days ordained for me were written in Your book before one of them came to be."
- Do not be overanxious for changes you see in your friends which you may not have experienced yet. Trust God that those changes *will* occur – but in His timing (which, in His sovereignty, He knows is best for you). In some ways, late maturity is a blessing.

C. Modesty

❖ For both guys and girls, what someone wears sends messages about him or her and can trigger unexpected (and often undesired) responses in members of the opposite sex.

- Spend some time talking through what types of clothing are appropriate and inappropriate for both boys and girls. All clothing sends some message, regardless of your intent.
- Girls need to understand that what they wear can provoke a sexual response in boys because males tend to be visually stimulated more than females. (Girls are often utterly clueless on this point!)
- However, boys, too, should make clothing choices with purity and modesty in mind. A boy's inappropriate clothing could arouse a girl, encourage her to dress in a similarly inappropriate way, and/or communicate to her that he is sexually motivated and oriented.

❖ Both sexes can dress fashionably and attractively without being trendy or sexy.

- Consider discussing Romans 14:21 in terms of the clothing one chooses to wear.
- Ask your child to give some examples of clothing in her own closet (or worn recently by someone you know) that, based on what she now knows, she would consider inappropriate. Discuss and try to reach agreement on what your family's standards will be in choosing what to buy and wear. Don't forget categories like bathing suits, special occasion clothing (i.e. a prom or a wedding), and sports/work-out clothing.
- Ask your child what it is that influences his clothing choices. Are those influences godly or ungodly?

D. Society's Overemphasis on Appearance

❖ In our culture, particularly in the teen years, a primary focus is outward appearance.

- Discuss how different forms of media (magazines, T.V., etc.) turn our focus toward the outward appearance, rather than the inner character of ourselves and other people.
- Talk about how we, too, all too often judge others by their appearance and/or possessions.

❖ God focuses on the *heart*, not outward appearances. [Read 1 Samuel 16:7 to discover what God said to Samuel about one of Jesse's older sons as he was choosing the next king of Israel from Jesse's family – "But the Lord said to Samuel, 'Do not consider his appearance or his height, for I have rejected him. The Lord does not look at the things man looks at. **Man looks at the outward appearance, but the Lord looks at the heart**'" (emphasis added).]

- Ask: "Can you think of any ways you might have gotten caught up in appearance and/or status in evaluating yourself or others recently? Consider how much time you spend on your physical appearance." (This will not be a problem for many boys☺, but some teens may discover that they are spending more time and energy worrying about what they look like than on more important things, like their inner character. For example, less time in front of the mirror before school could mean a longer or better quiet time in the morning!)

E. Romantic Books, Movies, and Music

- The books and magazines you read, the T.V. shows and movies you see, and the music you hear can strongly influence what you think and believe about love, sex, and marriage.

    - Discuss how your child's perception of male/female roles and relationships, romance, dating, marriage, and sex have been influenced by things he has read, heard, or seen. Ask: "In what ways are these perceptions unrealistic, and how could these be harmful to you?" (For example, in addition to the obvious dangers of seeing premarital sex on screen or a torrid love scene described in a book or song, the romances portrayed in these media, even if they are not immoral, often give a false and romanticized view of relationships and are likely to influence a teen's expectations for his or her own future experiences.)
    - Evaluate the types of books your family reads, movies you see, and music to which you listen. Ask your teen, "How can you safeguard yourself from developing unrealistic and/or worldly expectations of love, romance, sex, and marriage?"

- God wants us to allow only what is excellent and praiseworthy into our lives.

    - Read Philippians 4:8.

II. Sexual Love: What It Is and How It Works

- Ask: What do you already know about sexual intimacy and sexuality? What do you think and feel about sexual love? Do you understand the mechanics of how sexual love works/happens? Tell us what you know.

  Note to parents: This may take some time and gentle encouragement, but it is important to find out where your child is coming from, what he knows (or thinks he knows), and if there are any misconceptions already in his or her mind that you will need to correct. Consider asking direct questions about specific terms (i.e. masturbation, foreplay, orgasm) as a way to prompt sharing.

A. What Sexual Love Is:

- It is a gift from God to be enjoyed by one woman and one man, and only *after* having made a lifetime commitment to one another through marriage.
- It is an expression of love between a man and a woman that involves intense physical pleasure & excitement and deep emotional intimacy.
- It is a permanent bonding of souls on earth and is God's way of bringing children into the world in a way that best meets their needs.

B. What Sexual Love Is Not:

- Something dirty, wrong, or impure (when within appropriate boundaries)
- A mere physical activity pursued only for your own personal pleasure

C. How It Works:

Note to parents: Discuss some or all of the following body parts and their functions. Use the diagram in Appendix II to enhance your instruction if you feel the illustrations would be helpful.

❖ The Male Anatomy

- Penis
- Scrotum
- Testicles

❖ The Female Anatomy

- Breasts
- Vagina
- Clitoris
- Womb/uterus
- Ovaries/fallopian tubes

❖ Sexual Love

- Kissing (Foreplay)
- Caressing (Foreplay)
- Holding (Foreplay)
- Erection (male)/Arousal (female)
- Intercourse
- Orgasm*
- Semen
- Eggs-Ovaries-Ovulation
- Pregnancy

* *Note to parents*: If you feel that directly describing the experience of orgasm is not appropriate for your teen, either generally or at this age, then the illistrations listed below may help him understand a little bit about the physical and emotional aspects of an orgasm in less graphic detail. Orgasm is not something one can or should fully understand until one experiences it himself, and perhaps stating that, "you'll understand it when you experiance it" is explanation enough. But a particularly inquisitive child may push for more information. In such a case you might use the following illustrations:

- A sneeze – a period of anticipation, followed by an intense physical and emotional release
- The first hill of a roller coaster ride – slow period of build-up and anticipation followed by a wild rush of physical and emotional release
- With discretion, share Dad's experience as a male
- With discretion, share Mom's experience as a female

If you decide to share from your own experience, consider focusing primarily on the emotional effects of sexual intercourse. Discuss both the challenges and rewards of waiting until marriage for this experience.

III. CONCLUSIONS

- ❖ Sexual love is a wonderful gift from God, given to us to be enjoyed, but only within the marriage relationship.
  - We will address this fully in the next lesson.
- ❖ Sexual intercourse is a love-enhancing act where we freely give ourselves physically to someone to whom we have already given our hearts in a committed marriage relationship.
- ❖ Sexual love is a good thing protected by marriage, not a bad or evil thing prohibited except by marriage.

We are going to look at a number of other areas in the next couple of weeks, including:

- ✓ God's Design for Sex: Purity and Marriage
- ✓ Love vs. Lust and Infatuation
- ✓ Sexual Purity and Self-Control
- ✓ Whom and When Should I Date?
- ✓ A Covenant of Sexual Purity

- We want you to continue to come to us, rather than your friends or anyone else, with any questions you have about these topics. There is a lot of wrong information and many dangerous lies and myths that the media and the world try to pass off as truth to young people. Some of your friends may believe many of these lies – and thus, without meaning to, could give you wrong information. God has given us to you as parents and mentors to prepare you for adulthood in all areas – including sexual issues.
- We will always tell you the truth. And we will always try to help you understand life from God's perspective, based on what He says in the Bible.
- We will also follow up with you periodically during the next few years to talk about many of these issues and topics again, often in more detail than tonight, as your need for information and your maturity level increase.

IV. YOUR QUESTIONS

What are your thoughts and feelings about what we have just shared?
How does what we have talked about affect you today?
Are there questions you have that we haven't answered?
How will you respond to what you have learned in our discussion?

Note to parents: At the end of this session, review your expectations of your child for the study.

- Set a date for the next session.
- Give him the follow-up study and emphasize that it must be completed by the next session.
- Talk about how she could work the follow-up study into her schedule amidst her other commitments and activities (i.e. as part of her quiet time a couple of mornings a week, after school on a day or days that typically have lighter homework, over the weekend, etc.).
- Keep your tone positive, though serious, and express how much you are looking forward to the next session and to seeing his answers to the questions in the follow-up study.

Part 1B - Student Discussion Notes

I. Adolescence: A Period of Growth and Change in All Areas

Luke 2:52 – "And Jesus grew in wisdom (intellectually) and stature (physically), and in favor with God (spiritually) and men (socially)."

As you enter the teen years, you are growing and maturing just as Jesus did:

- ❖ Physically (height, strength, hormonal balance, etc.)
- ❖ Spiritually (Bible studies, corporate and personal worship, family devotions, personal quiet times, Sunday school class, etc.)
- ❖ Socially (school, youth group, sports, camps and retreats, etc.)
- ❖ Intellectually (school, clubs, etc.)

A. Changes in Adolescence

What kinds of physical, social, or emotional changes are you currently experiencing?

What kinds of physical, social, or emotional changes can you expect to experience in the next few months and years?

B. Timing of Adolescence

- ❖ Your own physical changes will occur in the special _______________ that God has designed just for _______________. (Psalm 139:13-16)

C. Modesty

❖ For both guys and girls, what someone ____________ sends messages about him or her and can trigger unexpected (and often undesired) ________________ in members of the opposite sex.

❖ Both sexes can dress _______________ and _______________ without being ___________ or ___________.

D. Society's Overemphasis on Appearance

❖ In our culture, and particularly in the teen years, a primary focus is outward ________________.

❖ God focuses on the ______________, not outward appearances. (1 Samuel 16:7)

E. Romantic Books, Movies, and Music

❖ The books and magazines you read, the T.V. shows and movies you see, and the music you hear can ______________________ influence what you think and believe about love, sex, and marriage.

❖ God wants us to allow only what is _____________ and ____________ into our lives. (Phil. 4:8)

How can you safeguard yourself from developing unrealistic and/or worldly expectations of love, sex, and marriage?

II. Sexual Love: What It Is and How It Works

A. What Sexual Love Is:

❖ It is a gift from God to be enjoyed only by one _____________ and one _____________, and only ____________ having made a lifetime commitment to one another through ____________.

❖ It is an expression of love between a man and a woman that involves intense ________________ pleasure & excitement and deep _______________ intimacy.

❖ It is a permanent _______________________ of souls on earth and is God's way of bringing ________________________ into the world in a way that best meets their needs.

B. What Sexual Love Is Not:

- ❖ Something ___________________, wrong, or impure (when within appropriate boundaries)
- ❖ A mere ______________ activity pursued only for your own personal __________________

C. How It Works:

- ❖ The Male Anatomy

- ❖ The Female Anatomy

- ❖ Sexual Love

III. CONCLUSIONS

- ❖ Sexual love is a wonderful ____________ from God, given to us to be enjoyed, but ____________ within the marriage relationship.

- ❖ Sexual intercourse is a ________-____________ act where we freely give ourselves physically to someone to whom we have already given our hearts in a committed _________________ relationship.

- ❖ Sexual love is a _____________ thing protected by marriage, not a _________ or ___________ thing prohibited except by marriage.

IV. YOUR QUESTIONS

What are your thoughts and feelings about what we have just shared?

How does what we have talked about affect you today?

Are there questions you have that we haven't answered?

How will you respond to what you have learned in our discussion?

Part 1C - Student Follow-up Study

Scripture Memory: *Ephesians 2:10, Jeremiah 29:11*

As you go through physical, emotional, and social changes during your adolescent years, you will likely feel very insecure at times about who you are and why you exist. In fact, this is probably one of the biggest challenges during the teen years. The following verses and questions help to remind us about our true identity and how it can help anchor us in these often confusing and challenging years.

1. Read John 1:12-13; 2 Corinthians 5:17; Ephesians 1:13-14.

   a. What do these verses tell us about who we are?

2. Read Ephesians 2:10.

   a. What do you think it means to be called God's workmanship?

   b. What does this mean to you personally?

   c. This verse ends by stating that we were "created in Christ Jesus to do good works, which God prepared in advance for us to do." How does this help you understand your true identity?

3. How, specifically, does remembering your true identity in Christ help you as you face the many challenges you will encounter during your teen years?

4. What questions or concerns do you want to discuss further with us?

Part 1D - Parent Follow-up Guide

Scripture Memory: *Ephesians 2:10, Jeremiah 29:11*

As you go through all these physical, emotional, and social changes during your adolescent years, you will likely feel very insecure at times about who you are and why you exist. In fact, this is probably one of the biggest challenges during the teen years. The following verses and questions help to remind us about our true identity and how it can help anchor us in these often confusing and challenging years.

1. **Read John 1:12-13; 2 Corinthians 5:17; Ephesians 1:13-14:**

   John 1:12-13 – "Yet to all who received Him, to those who believed in His name, He gave the right to become children of God – children born not of natural descent, nor of human decision or a husband's will, but born of God."

   2 Corinthians 5:17 – "Therefore, if anyone is in Christ, he is a new creation; the old has gone, the new has come!"

   Ephesians 1:13-14 – "And you also were included in Christ when you heard the word of truth, the gospel of your salvation. Having believed, you were marked in Him with a seal, the promised Holy Spirit, who is a deposit guaranteeing our inheritance until the redemption of those who are God's possession – to the praise of His glory."

   What do these verses tell us about who we are?
   - We are children of God.
   - When we accept Jesus as Savior, we are born again: We are new and changed in the very core of our being, so our identity is now that of children of the King and willing servants of Christ, rather than as slaves of sin.
   - Satan, the world, and our sin nature have power over us before we become a new creation in Christ. Satan relentlessly uses the world to exploit our sin nature.
   - When we are saved, God gives us the promise of a new life in Christ.
   - The Holy Spirit seals that promise, helps us to understand God's will for our lives, and empowers us to overcome sin and our sin nature on a daily basis.
   - Sin is no longer inevitable – it is a choice – because we now have the Spirit's power within us to deny the sin nature and gain victory over sin every day.

2. **Read Ephesians 2:10 –** "For we are God's workmanship, created in Christ Jesus to do good works, which God prepared in advance for us to do."

   What do you think it means to be called God's workmanship?
   - We are created by God's hands.
   - He has given each of us different bodies, personalities, abilities, status, intelligence, and spiritual gifts.
   - No one is a mistake; everyone is a masterpiece.
   - God created us for a unique and special purpose in this world that only we can fulfill.
   - He wants to use us just as we are to to have an intimate relationship with Him and to show His love to a fallen world. Through all of this, His ultimate goal is to bring glory to Himself.

- These truths are incredibly freeing and endow each of us with great value. When we are tempted to compare ourselves to others and to doubt our importance, usefulness, or purpose on this earth, we can stand with confidence on this foundation: God loves us as we are and had a special reason for creating us.

What does this mean to you personally?

Answers will vary from person to person but might include:

- I should be content with my body (size, height, weight, body type, skin, face, etc.), even its seeming flaws.
- I should be content with my intellectual abilities.
- I should remember that God created me to be just as I am today. He has a special and unique purpose for me *now* and in the future.
- God views me as a masterpiece, created for His pleasure, glory, and honor.
- Because God has a special purpose for my life, I can be joyful in the present and hopeful about the future, regardless of circumstances and any current personal flaws or limitations.
- Even hard and trying times, are appointed to me for God's purposes.

This verse ends by stating that we were "created in Christ Jesus to do good works, which God prepared in advance for us to do." How does this help you understand your true identity?

- We were created for a special purpose: to do God's will and to bring Him honor. Because we are grateful for our salvation and because we love God, we want to do the work He has planned uniquely for us since the beginning of time.
- I don't need to try to be like anyone else. God created *me*, especially to do a particular work or works and to glorify Him in a unique way. If I try to be like someone else, I will never live up to my full potential.

3. **How, specifically, does remembering your true identity in Christ help you as you face the many challenges you will encounter during your teen years?**

   Answers will vary from person to person but might include:

   - Our identity in Christ is the basis for our entire life. He created us just as we are for a special purpose. This identity provides us with an ultimate destiny for our entire life and, as a result, a reason for living each moment to its fullest in His service.
   - Because God created us, He cares about our whole self – emotional, physical, social, intellectual, and spiritual. He wants us to surrender every part of our lives to Him in order to bring greater glory to Him, which is our ultimate purpose.
   - When we remember our real identity – a child of God whose purpose is to bring greater glory to God in all things – our identity in Christ becomes like a compass and an anchor:

     As a **compass**, it gives you a specific direction for your life as you walk through the teen years and are tempted to follow other paths.

     As an **anchor**, it gives you something secure to hold onto when the storms and challenges and temptations of growing up in today's world threaten to push you off God's path.

4. **What questions or concerns do you want to discuss further with us?**

Session 2:

God's Design for Sexual Love-Purity When Single and Faithfulness When Married

Session Purpose and Themes

Session Summary:

This session emphasizes God's call to holiness and how Christians answer that call while single and in marriage. We discuss God's original design for marriage and how that design can be fulfilled even in a fallen world. We also introduce the concept of the "suitable" spouse (from Genesis 2), a theme which we will build upon in later sessions.

Session Themes:

- God commands that we pursue purity and holiness in all aspects of our lives. This includes how we use our minds and our bodies.
- God designed sexual love to be a "one flesh" relationship experienced only within the marriage relationship and only with that one "suitable" person that God has in store for us as our lifelong companion.
- God designed sexual love to be enjoyed by us within the marriage relationship. It should be unselfish and regular in marriage, focusing on satisfying the other's needs and desires before our own.

Hints for a More Effective Study

- Use this study as an opportunity to begin or continue what we hope will be a recurring discussion with your teen about the characteristics and character qualities which would make someone a "suitable" spouse for him. Because his choice of a spouse is one of the most important decisions he will make in his lifetime, encourage him to begin his preparation for that decision early. Making a list *now* of those character qualities he most desires in a spouse is a good initial step in this process. (This is one of the assignments made in the Session 2 Follow-Up Study.) This list will be valuable to revisit and revise regularly over the coming years as your teen approaches an age when he would consider marriage.
- Use the passages from Song of Songs to emphasize that, even (perhaps especially) for Christians, God designed sexual love to be an intensely exciting, pleasurable, and even erotic experience between a husband and a wife. Our culture is not necessarily wrong in acknowledging the erotic side of sexual love, but it is wrong to emphasize it exclusively and to do so outside the context of marriage and in ways that invite immoral thoughts and actions.
- During your discussion of the Student Follow-Up Study, emphasize the practical steps that you and your teen can take, both individually and together, to protect this special gift of sexual love for her as she progresses through the teenage years. Make a commitment to pray regularly for wisdom in protecting her from premature emotional and physical involvement with the opposite sex and in finding a "suitable" spouse.

Precautions

- If your teen has somehow received the impression that sex is "dirty," it is particularly important that you emphasize the positive aspects of a biblical one-flesh relationship. Reassure him that in your eyes, as well as in God's, sex between one man and one woman within the context of marriage is a beautiful and enjoyable thing.
- Be sure to caution your teen that in listing qualities she would like in a spouse, she is not creating a litmus test which any potential spouse must pass. No one could live up to the ideals that most of us create in our minds when we think of what we would like in a spouse! It is important, however, that your teen know what she is looking for and to discern over time which qualities on her list would be "non-negotiable" when she considers marriage.
- As parents, you know better than anyone else your teen's temperament, love language, strengths, weaknesses, and other needs – information which will be essential in his quest for a compatible spouse. Regardless of how large a role you wish to play in your teen's final selection of a spouse, you should share your insights into his needs.
- You can do this now, as you introduce the concept of "The List," or you might choose to wait and share your observations through the course of normal conversation. You will want choosing a "suitable" spouse to be a frequent topic of discussion in your home with all of your children.
- Use these conversations both to listen to your teen's desires and needs and to steer his thoughts in a direction that you know, through study in the Word, general life experience, and your intimate knowledge of him, is best.

Additional Resources

Chapman, Gary. *The Five Love Languages*. Chicago: Northfield Pub., 1992.

Chapman, Gary. *The Five Love Languages of Teenagers*. Chicago: Northfield Pub., 2000.

Gresh, Dannah. *And the Bride Wore White: Seven Secrets to Sexual Purity*. Chicago: Moody Publishers, 1999.

Leman, Kevin. *The Birth Order Connection: Finding and Keeping the Love of Your Life*. Grand Rapids: F.H. Revell, 2001.

Warren, Neil Clark. *Finding the Love of Your Life: Ten Principles for Choosing the Right Marriage Partner*. Colorado Springs: Focus on the Family, 1992.

The authors gratefully acknowledge the Rev. Jay Childs, pastor of Midland Evangelical Free Church, as a primary resource for the material in this session.

Part 2A - Parent Discussion Guide

***Introductory comments*:**

- As God originally designed it, sexual love is a beautiful and wonderful gift that is to be enjoyed only by one man and one woman, and only within the boundaries of a committed marriage relationship.
- When enjoyed in this way, it is an incredibly selfless expression of love between two people; however, because of his sinful nature, man has distorted and ignored God's original design for sexual love.
- In doing so, he has essentially turned sexual love into a perversion pursued outside of a committed marriage relationship, often with more than one partner over the course of a lifetime, and primarily for the individual's own self-gratification.
- In this study, we will briefly explore God's original overall design for sexual love, which is rooted in His command that we pursue holiness and purity in all aspects of our lives. By His design, sexual love is to be enjoyed regularly and to its fullest, but only in a committed marriage relationship between a man and a woman – not with anyone (including the person one intends to marry) *before* marriage and not with anyone else *after* marriage.

I. God commands purity and holiness in all aspects of our lives, including how we use our bodies.

❖ God has saved us and calls us to a <u>holy</u> life, which includes offering our <u>bodies</u> to Him as living sacrifices.

Read 2 Timothy 1:9 and Romans 12:1 :

2 Timothy 1:9 – "[God] has saved us and called us to a holy life – not because of anything we have done but because of His own purpose and grace. This grace was given us in Christ Jesus before the beginning of time. . . ."

Romans 12:1 – "Therefore, I urge you, brothers, in view of God's mercy, to offer your bodies as living sacrifices, holy and pleasing to God – this is your spiritual act of worship."

❖ Because our bodies and souls were bought at the cost of Christ's blood, they belong to God and are <u>temples</u> of the Holy Spirit. Therefore, we must learn to <u>control</u> our bodies in a way that is holy and honorable to God. This includes <u>fleeing</u> every sort of sexual immorality. (1 Corinthians 6:18-20)

Read 1 Corinthians 6:18-20 – "Flee from sexual immorality. All other sins a man commits are outside his body, but he who sins sexually sins against his own body. Do you not know that your body is a temple of the Holy Spirit, who is in you, whom you have received from God? You are not your own; you were bought at a price. Therefore honor God with your body."

II. Sexual love is to be experienced only within the marriage relationship.

Read Genesis 2:20-24, Matthew 19:4-9, and Ephesians 5:22-33.

What do these verses tell us about God's design and intentions for marriage?

❖ God intends each of us to marry someone who is "suitable" for us. (Genesis 2:20b)

- God created Eve to be a "suitable" wife for Adam, someone who completed him in a way only she could.

- A husband and wife were designed to be each other's completers, in a relationship designed to unite their bodies, hearts, minds, and lives and in which each is "suited" for (uniquely compatible or complementary to) the other.

- One primary purpose of a marriage is to honor God, by enabling two indiviuals to do more together to glorify and serve Him than either could do alone. Thus, a "suitable" person is someone who will enhance your ability to bring glory and honor to God.

- Being married holds up our lives to the most intense of mirrors and helps us to see our own faults through the eyes of our spouse. Marriage thus enables us, with the power of the Holy Spirit, to attempt to improve these areas of weakness. A "suitable" spouse should be able to hold up the mirror for us in a constructive, loving way.

- Being married helps us better to understand the entire character of God, both masculine and feminine traits. (For two examples of how God demonstrates both masculine and feminine qualities, see Psalm 24:8 and Isaiah 66:13. There are many other examples throughout Scripture.)

❖ God designed marriage as a "one flesh" relationship with three distinct aspects that are symbolized in the marriage ceremony (Genesis 2:24):

1. Leave – A man and a woman each leave their parents.
2. Cleave – A man and a woman are united to each other.
3. Weave – A man and a woman become "one flesh" (physically, emotionally, and spiritually).

- The "one flesh" literally refers to the act of sex, which mysteriously creates a union between a man and a woman that is both physical and spiritual. The husband and wife become one.

- That is one reason why Jesus says in Matthew 19:6 that " 'there are no longer two, but one'" and "'what God has joined together, let man not separate.' "

- That is also why Paul writes in 1 Corinthians 6:16 that, "one who unites himself with a prostitute is one with her in body."

- However, you need to understand that, while the act of having sex creates a physical "one flesh" relationship, the intimacy of marriage has other, equally important dimensions (intellectual, emotional, and spiritual).

❖ God <u>created</u> marriage and intended it for <u>one</u> man and <u>one</u> woman, for a lifetime. (Matthew 19:4-6)

- In Matthew 19, Jesus recites God's account of marriage at the time of creation and confirms God's intention that it be permanent by adding, " 'Therefore, what God has joined together, let man not separate.' "

- Note also in Genesis 2:22 that *God brought* Eve, a woman, to Adam as his unique and "suitable" helper.

- Note also in Matthew 19:8-9 that Jesus tells the Pharisees that God permitted divorce only because of man's sinfulness (hard heart). He also tells them that getting divorced and marrying someone else, except in the case of marital unfaithfulness, is adultery. Marriage was designed to be permanent. (See also Malachi 2:16 – " 'I hate divorce,' says the Lord God of Israel.")

❖ Marriage is a visible <u>symbol</u> of Christ's relationship to the church. (Ephesians 5:22-33)

- Christ is the husband/groom; the church is the wife/bride.

- The husband loves and sacrifices himself for his wife as Christ did for the Church. The wife submits in reverance to her husband, as the church does to Christ.

Note to parents: Now would be an appropriate time to share your own thoughts on the one- flesh relationship, including how the physical relationship must be complemented by other forms of intimacy for a marriage to be complete and mutually fulfilling.

III. God created sex for us to enjoy.

Read Song of Songs 2:3-13 and 4:1-15.

- Note that chapter 2 is a song from a woman to her husband and chapter 4 is a song from a man to his wife.

What kind of picture do these passages give you about the kind of sexual love that God intends for a man and a woman in marriage?

Note the following:

2:3b – " I delight to sit in his shade, and his fruit is sweet to my taste."
2:10 – " My lover spoke and said to me, 'Arise, my darling, my beautiful one, and come with me.' "
4:1a – " How beautiful you are, my darling! Oh, how beautiful!"
4:10 – " How delightful is your love, my sister, my bride! How much more pleasing is your love than wine, and the fragrance of your perfume than any spice!"

Sexual love is a wonderful, fun, and exciting aspect of marriage!

IV. Sexual love should be unselfish and regular in marriage.

Read 1 Corinthians 7:1-5 – "Now for the matters you wrote about: It is good for a man not to marry. But since there is so much immorality, each man should have his own wife, and each woman her own husband. The husband should fulfill his marital duty to his wife, and likewise the wife to her husband. The wife's body does not belong to her alone but also to her husband. In the same way, the husband's body does not belong to him alone but also to his wife. Do not deprive each other except by mutual consent and for a time, so that you may devote yourselves to prayer. Then come together again so that Satan will not tempt you because of your lack of self-control."

What do these verses tell us about what a husband's and a wife's attitudes toward sexual love in marriage should be?

❖ A husband and a wife should focus first on satisfying the <u>other's</u> sexual needs.

- In general, a man desires <u>physical</u> satisfaction most from sexual love.
- In general, a woman desires <u>romance</u> and <u>emotional</u> <u>closeness</u> most from sexual love.
- This means that a man will have to think beyond his own desires to give his wife what she needs and wants in their sexual relationship, and the woman will have to think beyond her own desires to give her husband what he needs and wants from their sexual relationship.

❖ Sexual love should be a <u>regular</u> activity in the marriage relationship.

- Note v. 5a – "Do not deprive each other except by mutual consent and for a time. . . ."

Conclusion

Sexual love is a good thing protected by marriage, not a bad thing prohibited except by marriage. It creates a "one flesh" relationship that is to be enjoyed *only* within the marriage relationship, not beforehand with anyone and not with anyone else after marriage.

Part 2B - Student Discussion Notes

I. God commands purity and holiness in all aspects of our lives, including how we use our bodies.

❖ God has saved us and calls us to a ___________ life, which includes offering our ___________ to Him as living sacrifices. (2 Timothy 1:9; Romans 12:1)

❖ Because our bodies and souls were bought at the cost of Christ's blood, they belong to God and are ________________ of the Holy Spirit. Therefore, we must learn to ________________ our bodies in a way that is holy and honorable to God. This includes ___________ every sort of sexual immorality. (1 Corinthians 6:18-20)

II. Sexual love is to be experienced only within the marriage relationship.

Read Genesis 2:20-24, Matthew 19:4-9, and Ephesians 5:22-33.

What do these verses tell us about God's design and intentions for marriage?

❖ God intends for each of us to marry someone who is "___________" for us. (Genesis 2:20b)

❖ God designed marriage as a "________ ___________" relationship with three distinct aspects that are symbolized in the marriage ceremony (Genesis 2:24):

1. ______________ – A man and a woman each leave their parents.

2. ______________ – A man and a woman are united to each other.

3. ______________ – A man and a woman become "one flesh" (physically, emotionally, and spiritually).

❖ God ___________ marriage and intended it for ___________ man and ___________ woman, for a lifetime. (Matthew 19:4-6)

❖ Marriage is a visible ______________ of Christ's relationship to the church. (Ephesians 5:22-33)

III. God created sex for us to enjoy.

Read Song of Songs 2:3-13 and 4:1-15.

What kind of picture do these passages give you about the kind of sexual love that God intends for a man and a woman in marriage?

Sexual love is a wonderful, fun, and exciting aspect of marriage!

IV. Sexual love should be unselfish and regular in marriage.

Read 1 Corinthians 7:1-5.

What do these verses tell us about what a husband's and a wife's attitudes toward sexual love in marriage should be?

❖ A husband and a wife should focus first on satisfying the ____________ sexual needs.

- In general, a man desires _______________ satisfaction most from sexual love.

- In general, a woman desires ___________ and _____________ _____________ most from sexual love.

❖ Sexual love should be a _____________ activity in the marriage relationship.

Conclusion

Sexual love is a good thing protected by marriage, not a bad thing prohibited except by marriage. It creates a "one flesh" relationship that is to be enjoyed *only* within the marriage relationship, not beforehand with anyone and not with anyone else after marriage.

Part 2C - Student Follow-up Study

Scripture Memory: *Genesis 2:23-24, Matthew 19:4-6*

1. Based on our study together, why is sexual love to be enjoyed only within a marriage relationship?

2. Read the story of Boaz and Ruth (in Ruth 3 and 4) as an illustration of a marriage where two people followed God's design for marriage and sexual love. Summarize briefly what happened.

   What were the results for Ruth, Boaz, and their descendents for following God's design?

3. Read the story of David and Bathsheba (2 Samuel 11) as an illustration of a sexual relationship that did not follow God's design for marriage and sexual love. Summarize briefly what happened.

   What were the results for David and Bathsheba and their descendents for not following God's design? (Read 2 Samuel 12:10-12; 12:15-18; and 16:21-22.)

4. Think about some characteristics that would make someone "suitable" for you as a spouse. Or stated another way – what would your ideal mate be like?

5. How, specifically, can you protect the special gift of sexual love which God has given you, starting today?

6. How, specifically, can we as your parents pray for these things for you today? How, specifically, can you pray for these things yourself?

7. What questions or concerns do you want to discuss further with us?

Part 2D - Parent Follow-up Guide

Scripture Memory: *Genesis 2:23-24, Matthew 19:4-6*

1. **Based on our study together, why is sexual love to be enjoyed only within a marriage relationship?**

- God's command that we be holy and pure extends to how we use our minds and bodies. (2 Timothy 1:9 and Romans 12:1)
- God, in His wisdom, designed it this way for our own good. (Matthew 19:4-9) God hates divorce. (Malachi 2:16) We can always trust God's commands.

Note to parents: If you wish, you could discuss here some of the practical benefits of keeping sex within the bounds of marriage (i.e. avoiding sexually transmitted diseases, children conceived out of wedlock, etc.) as further evidence of God's wisdom and trustworthiness.

- Sex between a man and a woman creates a mysterious physical and spiritual "one flesh" relationship between them. (Genesis 2:24; Matthew 19:5; and 1 Corinthians 6:16) This gives sex spiritual, as well as physical and emotional, significance.

2. **Read the story of Boaz and Ruth (in Ruth 3 and 4) as an illustration of a marriage where two people followed God's design for marriage and sexual love. Summarize briefly what happened.**

   What were the results for Ruth, Boaz, and their descendents for following God's design?

- They were honored and blessed by others in the town for following God's design. (4:11-12)
- They also became the grandparents of King David (4:18-22) and part of Jesus' lineage. (Matthew 1:1-16)

3. **Read the story of David and Bathsheba (2 Samuel 11) as an illustration of a sexual relationship that did not follow God's design for marriage and sexual love. Summarize briefly what happened.**

   What were the results for David and Bathsheba and their descendents for not following God's design? (Read 2 Samuel 12:10-12; 12:15-18; and 16:21-22.)

- David was chastised severely by God for his sin:
    1. The sword never left his house. (His descendants suffered constant strife and war – foretold in 2 Samuel 12:10 and carried out by God throughout the Old Testament.)
    2. His son Absalom had sex with his father's concubines in front of all Israel. (2 Samuel 12:11-12 and 16:21-22)
    3. His son from his extra-marital relationship with Bathsheba died. (2 Samuel 12:15-18)

4. **Think about some characteristics that would make someone "suitable" for you as a spouse. Or stated another way – what would your ideal mate be like?**

   Answers will vary from person to person but might include:
   - A vital personal relationship with Jesus Christ; spiritual maturity
   - A good sense of humor
   - Physical attraction
   - Intelligence
   - A strong work ethic
   - Compatible doctrinal beliefs
   - A healthy relationship with parents
   - A positive attitude in difficult circumstances
   - An ability to lead/follow in his/her God-given role
   - Characterized by respect for others, including me
   - Was raised in a home that modeled a strong marriage. (Note that you can often learn a lot by watching how his/her father and mother treat each other.)

5. **How, specifically, can you protect the special gift of sexual love which God has given you, starting today?**

   Answers will vary from person to person but might include:
   - I can commit to waiting for marriage for sexual activity of any kind. The same commitment and self-control one needs for this before marriage (purity) will be necessary in order to remain faithful to one's spouse after marriage (faithfulness).
   - If I date, explain my commitment to those I date. (See Session 5.)
   - Be accountable to others for my commitment.

6. **How, specifically, can we as your parents pray for these things for you today? How, specifically, can you pray for these things yourself?**

   Answers will vary from person to person but might include:
   - Pray for my choice of a mate – the person God created as a "suitable" life partner for me, consistent with His will for my life.
   - Pray for the character of my future spouse and for his or her parents in diligently training him or her to be a man or a woman of God. Pray for the protection of his or her purity.
   - Pray for the development of my character in becoming a "suitable" mate.
   - Pray for God's timing in meeting and developing a relationship with my future spouse. Pray for me to be patient in waiting for God's provision.
   - Pray for my purity before marriage and for my faithfulness after marriage.

7. **What questions or concerns do you want to discuss further with us?**

Session 3:

Infatuation and Lust vs.True Love

Session Purpose and Themes

Session Summary:

Session 3 explores what the Bible has to say on the topic of love. What is true love? How can you distinguish between love and infatuation? What is lust and why is it so dangerous? We address these questions in the context of a variety of Scriptures, including the illustrations used by Paul to instruct men in how to love their wives and the exhortations of Peter and Timothy to women on how to respect their husbands. Your teen will see that God's definition of love differs greatly from the kind of "love" we see glamorized in our culture.

Session Themes:

- There is an important difference between infatuation/lust and true love. It is at times hard to distinguish between them – particularly when you are young and inexperienced; yet the ability to discern the difference is essential if a teen is to avoid dishonoring God and making decisions and commitments that she may later regret.
- The Bible tells us to pursue true love (a selfless, deep, heart-level love that puts the interests of others above our own) and to avoid lust and infatuation (a surface- level, temporary, worldly, and self-centered desire that is never satisfied and ultimately leads to destruction and death).
- In the context of marriage, spouses are to pursue the model of selfless, other-oriented love described in 1 Corinthians 13 and modeled by Christ in His love for the Church (1 John 3:16).

Hints for a More Effective Study

- When discussing the differences between infatuation/lust and true love, try to be as concrete as you can by offering examples from real life, either public figures (like movie stars or athletes) and/or you and your own family, friends, and acquaintances. This should help make what are otherwise fairly abstract concepts more real to your teen and enhance his understanding of the truths you are discussing.
- If appropriate, share some of your own experiences with love and infatuation. Consider relating situations in which you pursued lust or infatuation because you confused it with true love and later regretted it. On the flip side, ask your teen if she can give examples of situations in which you and your spouse (or others you know) have demonstrated biblical, sacrificial love for one another as husband and wife.

Additional Resources

Harris, Joshua. *Boy Meets Girl: Say Hello to Courtship*. Sisters, Oregon: Multnomah Publishers, 2000.

Love & Respect Conference. Video, DVD, or CD. Emerson Eggrichs. Available from www.loveandrespect.com.

Part 3A - Parent Discussion Guide

***Introductory comments*:**

- In your teenage years, it is easy to confuse infatuation and lust with true love. But it is critical to distinguish between them, so that you don't dishonor God and later regreat decisions or commitments that were based simply on feelings or selfish desires .
- In this study, we will explore the differences between infatuation/lust and true love, what the Bible says about them, and why these differences are important for a healthy, godly perspective on love, sex, and marriage.

I. Defining Infatuation, Lust, and Love

- ❖ **Infatuation** – A self-centered, short-term attraction to someone whom you don't know well
- ❖ **Lust** – Selfish, excessive sexual craving that desires immediate gratification and that may turn to disgust when physically satisfied
- ❖ **Love** – An other-focused, permanent, heart-level connection that involves caring unconditionally and sacrificially for someone whom you know intimately

	Infatuation/Lust	**Love**
Focus	self-centered (for your own benefit)	other-focused (for their benefit)
Emphasis	surface level, outward focus (appearance)	heart level, inward focus (character)
Timing	short-lived, temporary	lasting, permanent
Origin	selfish, natural desires (sin nature)	heart concern for other (based on God's love for you)
Depth	surface (knowing *about* someone)	deep (*knowing* someone)

Examples :

- Consider discussing your own relationship (to the extent that at some point certain aspects of it may not have been based on true love).
- Most of what your teen sees of boy-girl relationships at his school or on the street are driven by lust or infatuation, not true love. It is obvious from the way many boys and girls hang all over one another that their primary interest is physical gratification.
- Discuss examples from your or your child's own experience with friends of the difference between "knowing *about* someone" when they started out as acquaintances and "*knowing*" someone after developing a friendship over time.

- Most Hollywood/tabloid romances are good examples of lust and/or infatuation. (We know these relationships usually are not true love because they don't last long; famous people frequently flit from one relationship to another.)
- Ask for any other examples your child can provide.

II. What the Bible Says about Infatuation and Lust

❖ It is never satisfied; it always wants more. (Proverbs 27:20)

Proverbs 27:20 – "Death and Destruction are never satisfied, and neither are the eyes of man."

❖ It is worldly; it is not from God. (1 John 2:16)

1 John 2:16 – "For everything in the world – the cravings of sinful man, the lust of his eyes and the boasting of what he has and does – comes not from the Father but from the world."

❖ It significantly limits our relationship with God. (Ephesians 4:18-19; 1 Peter 3:7)

Ephesians 4:18-19 – "They are darkened in their understanding and separated from the life of God because of the ignorance that is in them due to the hardening of their hearts. Having lost all sensitivity, they [Gentiles] have given themselves over to sensuality so as to indulge in every kind of impurity, with a continual lust for more."

1 Peter 3:7 – "Husbands, in the same way be considerate as you live with your wives, and treat them with respect as the weaker partner and as heirs with you of the gracious gift of life, **so that nothing will hinder your prayers**." (emphasis added)

❖ It leads to destruction and death. (Proverbs 7:25-27)

Proverbs 7:25-27 –
"Do not let your heart turn to [the adultress's] ways or stray into her paths.
Many are the victims she has brought down; her slain are a mighty throng.
Her house is a highway to the grave, leading down to the chambers of death."

❖ We should avoid it at all costs. (Proverbs 6:25; Colossians 3:5; Proverbs 4:23)

Proverbs 6:25 – "Do not lust in your heart after her beauty or let her captivate you with her eyes. . . ."

Colossians 3:5 – "Put to death, therefore, whatever belongs to your earthly nature: sexual immorality, impurity, lust, evil desires and greed, which is idolatry."

Proverbs 4:23 – "Above all else, guard your heart, for it is the wellspring of life."

III. What the Bible Says about True Love

Three kinds of love:

❖ **Eros** – an emotional and sexual desire, often erotic, for another

Examples: David and Bathsheba (2 Samuel 11:1-4)
Much of what we see in magazines, in movies, and on TV

❖ **Phileo** – a fond, non-sexual affection or mutual attraction based on common interests or insights

Examples: Jonathan and David (1 Samuel 20:17)
Siblings and friends

❖ **Agape** – a selfless love that puts the interests of others above your own

- It is modeled in the selfless love that Jesus showed through His suffering, death, and resurrection to provide forgiveness for our sins. (John 15:12-13)

  John 15:12-13 – " 'My command is this: Love each other as I have loved you. Greater love has no one than this, that he lay down his life for his friends.' "

- It is a love that often involves an act of will rather than feelings. (1 John 3:17-18)

  1 John 3:17-18 – "If anyone has material possessions and sees his brother in need but has no pity on him, how can the love of God be in him? Dear children, let us not love with words or tongue but with actions and in truth."

- It involves the same sort of self-sacrificing love for others that Jesus has shown to you. (1 John 3:16)

  1 John 3:16 – "This is how we know what love is: Jesus Christ laid down His life for us. And we ought to lay down our lives for our brothers."

Read 1 Corinthians 13:4-8. List some of the primary characteristics of true (or agape) love.
- Patient and kind (v. 4)
- Not envious, boastful or proud (v. 4)
- Neither rude nor self-seeking (v. 5)
- Not easily angered and keeps no record of wrongs (v. 5)
- Shuns evil and rejoices in the truth (v. 6)
- Always protects, trusts, hopes, perseveres (v. 7)
- TRUE LOVE NEVER FAILS (v. 8)

How do these characteristics make true love different from lust or infatuation?

- True love is very different from lust and infatuation:
  - ❖ True love strikes at a deeper level of relationship (the heart), and its focus is always on what is best for the other person.
  - ❖ By contrast, lust and infatuation are on a surface level (appearances) and are primarily concerned with the satisfaction of selfish desires, often at the expense of the other person.

Read Eph. 5:25-30. List the two examples husbands are given concerning how to love their wives:

- As Christ loved the church (5:25)
- As a man loves his own body (5:28)

For each example, list the kinds of actions that would be taken in each illustration, then how this would parallel practical actions to take towards a wife. (For example, in loving the church, Christ made one of His goals her holiness; a man could do this by encouraging his wife's spiritual growth. Or in caring for his own body, a man would treat any wounds or injuries he received; he could do this for his wife by listening to her troubles, fears, and worries and by asking her forgiveness when he hurts her by something he did or said.)

Example	**Actions Taken**	**Similar Actions for Wife**
1. Christ's Love for the Church	Gave His life for her	Give up one's own life/desires for her benefit
	Does what is best for her	Make choices and take actions that are best for her
	Pursues her "radiance"	Do things to promote her external and internal "radiance"
	His goal is her holiness	Encourage spiritual growth
2. Man's Love for His Own Body	Wash and clean it	Help her express her inner and outer beauty
	Feed it nutritious food	Make sure physical, emotional, and spiritual needs are met
	Exercise, build it up	Compliment and encourage her
	Give it good rest	Carry her burdens and share her work
	Treat/heal wounds and injuries	Listen to her fears and worries; seek forgiveness when you hurt her

How would this kind of love differ from infatuation or lust in terms of how you would treat your spouse in marriage?

- Again, it is other-oriented and focuses on the deeper, heart-level needs of the other person rather than on one's own selfish desires and expectations.

Read 1 Peter 3:1-6 and 1 Timothy 2:9-10. What do these passages suggest as ways that a woman can develop true beauty and demonstrate true love for her husband?

- Demonstrate respect for her husband, even if he is not a godly man (1 Peter 3:1-2)
- Do not preach or nag, but let her loving actions speak for her (1 Peter 3:1)

- Seek to exemplify purity and reverence in her life (for example, not gossiping or listening to gossip, building others up instead of tearing them down, wearing modest clothing, meditating on Scripture, demonstrating a fear of God in her worship and daily life) (1 Peter 3:2)
- Pray for and seek to develop the character qualities of gentleness and inner peace (1 Peter 1:4)
- Focus more on the beautifying of her inner self than on thinking about, shopping for, and adorning her outward self with clothes and jewelry (1 Peter 1:3-4); focusing on good deeds, rather than fashion (1 Timothy 2:9-10)
- Do not give in to fear; instead, trust God to work in her husband's life without her interference (1 Peter 3:5-6)

How would these qualities and actions by a woman inspire true love, rather than lust/infatuation?

- They draw attention to her character, rather than her body.
- They provide the foundation for a love that lasts – love that can withstand difficult circumstances and the tests of time, long after physical beauty has faded.
- They point to the author of True Love and the way to the ultimate love relationship.

Conclusion: Learn to distinguish between lust/infatuation and true love. When considering a possible relationship with someone of the opposite sex, make sure you are motivated by true and selfless (agape) love rather than self-centered lust or infatuation.

IV. Application to Me Today

Understanding what you now do about the difference between infatuation/lust and true love, what kinds of things ("indicators") will you look for in your future relationships with the opposite sex that will help you know whether you are motivated by infatuation/lust or true love?

- Give relationships time to develop and deepen. This allows you to *know* the other person rather than simply *know about* the other person. Real love is not in a hurry.
- Focus on the heart – the person's character qualities (both positive and negative), how the person relates to God, his family, and authorities in his life, what his actions (more than his words) tell you about his priorities and values.
- Be realistic about what you have in common and how you are different. When the first blush of romantic love fades, there has to be something stronger than physical attraction to hold you together through the inevitable ups and downs of life.
- Is God still first in your relationship? Real love puts God first. You help the one you love the most by putting God first.
- Ask yourself what your motives are and/or why you are interested in the other person:
  - Is it primarily physical attraction?
  - Is it the idea of being loved and desired?
  - Is it the status that association with this person affords you?
  - Is it how you feel when you are with them? Or is it something deeper?
  - Do they demonstrate character qualities that you admire?
  - Does their personality complement yours?
  - Do they share your values, goals, and passion for God?
  - Do they inspire you to a higher standard?
  - Do they have the kind of inner beauty that will withstand the test of time?
  - Are they the kind of person you could lead (male) or be led by (female)?
  - Are they well-liked by people you respect and trust?

Part 3B - Student Discussion Notes

I. Defining Infatuation, Lust, and Love

- Infatuation – A self-centered, short-term ______________ to someone whom you don't know well

- Lust – A selfish, excessive sexual craving that desires ___________ gratification that may turn to _____________ when physically satisfied

- Love – An other-focused, permanent, heart-level connection that involves caring __________________ and__________________ for someone whom you know intimately

	Infatuation/Lust	Love
Focus		
Emphasis		
Timing		
Origin		
Depth		

Examples:

II. What the Bible Says about Infatuation and Lust

- It is never ___________; it always wants more. (Proverbs 27:20)

- It is _________; it is not from ___________. (1 John 2:16)

- It significantly ______________ our relationship with God. (Ephesians 4:18-19; 1 Peter 3:7)

❖ It leads to _______________ and ____________. (Proverbs 7:25-27)

❖ We should _______________ it at all costs. (Proverbs 6:25; Colossians 3:5; Proverbs 4:23)

III. What the Bible Says about True Love

Three kinds of love:

❖ **Eros** – An emotional and sexual desire, often erotic, for another

Examples:

❖ **Phileo** – a fond, non-sexual affection or mutual attraction based on common interests or insights

Examples:

❖ **Agape** – a selfless love that puts the interests of others above your own

- It is _______________ in the selfless love that Jesus showed through His suffering, death, and resurrection to provide forgiveness for our sins. (John 15:12-13)
- It is a love that often involves an act of __________ rather than _____________. (1 John 3:17-18)
- It involves the same sort of ___________ - __________ love for others that Jesus has shown to you. (1 John 3:16)

Read 1 Corinthians 13:4-8. List some of the primary characteristics of true (or agape) love:

How do these characteristics make true love different from lust or infatuation?

Read Ephesians 5:25-30. List the two examples husbands are given concerning how to love their wives:

For each example, list the kinds of actions that would be taken in each illustration, then how this would parallel practical actions to take towards a wife.

Example	Actions Taken	Similar Actions for Wife
1.	a.	a.
	b.	b.
	c.	c.
	d.	d.
2.	a.	a.
	b.	b.
	c.	c.
	d.	d.

How would this kind of love differ from infatuation or lust in terms of how you would treat your spouse in marriage?

Read 1 Peter 3:1-6 and 1 Timothy 2:9-10. What do these passages suggest as ways that a woman can develop true beauty and demonstrate true love for her husband?

How would these qualities and actions by a woman inspire true love, rather than lust/infatuation?

Conclusion: Learn to distinguish between lust/infatuation and true love. When considering a possible relationship with someone of the opposite sex, make sure you are motivated by true and selfless (agape) love rather than self-centered lust or infatuation.

IV. Application to Me Today

Understanding what you now do about the difference between infatuation/lust and true love, what kinds of things ("indicators") will you look for in your future relationships with the opposite sex that will help you know whether you are motivated by infatuation/lust or true love?

Part 3C - Student Follow-up Study

Scripture Memory: *1 Corinthians 13:4-8*

1. In Proverbs, Solomon describes two different women, the "adulteress" (Proverbs 7:6-23) and the "wife of noble character" (Proverbs 31:10-31). The adulteress is actually a good example of a woman who attracts a man driven by infatuation and lust, and the wife of noble character is a good description of a woman who inspires true love in her husband.

   For the "adulteress," list the phrases (with verses) that illustrate that it is a relationship based on lust/infatuation.

   For the "wife of noble character," list the phrases (with verses) that illustrate that it is a relationship based on true love (that the husband knows his wife on more than a surface or appearance level).

2. The following story is a good example of a man who was driven by lust/infatuation in his relationship with a woman. Provide the details that show it was infatuation/lust vs. true love and describe the results of his decision to pursue infatuation/lust rather than true love.

   Amnon and Tamar (2 Samuel 13:1-22)

3. The story of Boaz & Ruth is a good example of a relationship marked by true love. Provide the details that show it was true love vs. infatuation/lust and the results of the decision to pursue true love instead of infatuation/lust.

   Boaz and Ruth (Ruth 2 and 3)

4. What questions or concerns do you want to discuss further with us?

Part 3D - Parent Follow-up Guide

Scripture Memory: *1 Corinthians 13:4-8*

1. **In Proverbs, Solomon describes two different women, the "adulteress" (Proverbs 7:6-23) and the "wife of noble character" (Proverbs 31:10-31). The adulteress is actually a good example of a woman who attracts a man driven by infatuation and lust, and the wife of noble character is a good description of a woman who inspires true love in her husband.**

   For the "adulteress," list the phrases (with verses) that illustrate that it is a relationship based on lust/infatuation.

   - "a youth who lacked judgment" (v. 7) [someone with weak character or in over his head]
   - a woman "dressed like a prostitute and with crafty intent" (v. 10) [immodest clothing; carnal character]
   - "she took hold of him and kissed him" (v. 13) [impulsive actions; physical intimacy without commitment]
   - She said, "I came out to meet you; I looked for you and have found you" (v. 15) [selfish focus on "I"]
   - She said, "I have covered my bed with colored linens from Egypt. I have perfumed my bed with myrrh, aloes and cinnamon" (v. 16) [focus on pleasures of the physical senses]
   - She said, "Come, let's drink deep of love until morning; let's enjoy ourselves with love" (v. 18) [short-term interest ("until morning"); physical intimacy without commitment]
   - She said, "My husband is not at home; he is on a long journey . . . and will not be home till full moon" (vv. 19-20) [short-term interest; unfaithful character]
   - "with persuasive words she led him astray; she seduced him with her smooth talk" (v. 21) [deceptive words, rather than truth-revealing actions]
   - "all at once he followed her like an ox going to the slaughter" (v. 22) [weak character; impulsive, with no thought for potential consequences]

   For the "wife of noble character," list the phrases (with verses) that illustrate that it is a relationship based on true love (that the husband knows his wife on more than a surface or appearance level).

   - "a wife of noble character" (v. 10) [heart level focus; inner beauty/character]
   - "her husband has full confidence in her and lacks nothing of value" (v. 11) [depth – *knowing* someone]
   - "She brings him good, not harm all the days of her life" (v. 12) [long-lasting; other- focused]
   - She "works with eager hands" (v. 13) [heart-level focus; inner beauty/character revealed in her actions]
   - "She gets up while it is still dark; she provides food for her family" (v. 15) [heart-level focus; inner beauty/character revealed in her actions]
   - "She considers a field and buys it; out of her earnings she plants a vineyard" (v. 16) [thinking long-term; making decisions after careful thought]

- “She sets about her work vigorously; her arms are strong for her tasks” (v. 17) [heart-level focus; inner beauty/character revealed in her attitude and actions]
- “She sees that her trading is profitable, and her lamp does not go out at night (v. 18) [heart-level focus; inner beauty/character]
- “She opens her arms to the poor and extends her hands to the needy” (v. 20) [other- focused]
- “She is clothed with strength and dignity; she can laugh at the days to come” (v. 25) [heart-level focus; inner beauty/character; thinking long-term]
- “She speaks with wisdom, and faithful instruction is on her tongue” (v. 26) [heart-level focus; inner beauty/character; words backed up by actions]
- “She watches over the affairs of her household and does not eat the bread of idleness” (v. 27) [heart-level focus; inner beauty/character revealed in actions; other-focused]
- “Her children arise and call her blessed; her husband also, and he praises her” (v. 28) [heart-level focus; inner beauty/character demonstrated in daily living; depth – her family *knows* her]
- “[A] woman who fears the Lord is to be praised” (v. 30) [inner beauty/character]

2. The following story is a good example of a man who was driven by lust/infatuation in his relationship with a woman. Provide the details that show it was infatuation/lust vs. true love and describe the results of his decision to pursue infatuation/lust rather than true love.

Amnon and Tamar (2 Samuel 13:1-22)

- Amnon fell in love with (desired) Tamar, beautiful sister of Absalom (v. 1) [focus on outward appearance]
- He became frustrated to the point of illness (v. 2) [obsessive focus; self-oriented]
- It seemed impossible to approach her for sexual gratification (v. 2) [desire for physical relationship without commitment]
- He schemed to get her alone to have sex with her (vv. 3-5) [focus on physical relationship]
- He would not listen to Tamar’s reasons for waiting (vv. 12-14) [self-centered focus]
- Because he was stronger than she, he raped her (v. 14) [self-centered focus; total disregard for the law, the long-term good of his family, and Tamar’s well-being and reputation]
- He hated her afterward, with even more hatred than he had “loved” her (v. 15) [short-lived, temporary emotions]
- Amnon’s actions planted the seeds of hate in Absalom (v. 22) which would later cause him to take Amnon’s life (2 Samuel 13:26-29) and left Tamar a “desolate woman,” without reputation or future (v. 20). It also contributed to the strained relationship between Absalom and his father, King David, which eventually led to civil war in Israel. (2 Samuel 15-18)

3. The story of Boaz & Ruth is a good example of a relationship marked by true love. Provide the details that show it was true love vs. infatuation/lust and the results of the decision to pursue true love instead of infatuation/lust.

Boaz and Ruth (Ruth 2 and 3)

- Boaz “courted” in a manner consistent with local custom and requirements of the law (entire text) [depth – getting to *know* someone; thinking holistically and long-term instead of acting impulsively on one’s own desires]
- Boaz made special efforts to care for Ruth and protect her (2:9) [other-focused]

- Boaz was impressed with her character (she stayed with her widowed mother-in-law; she worked hard in the fields) and her faith (she turned her back on her own culture's gods and acknowledged the one true God) (2:11-12) [heart-level focus; inner beauty; other-focused]
- Naomi noticed the character of Boaz (2:19) [depth – *knowing* someone; heart-level focus; inner beauty/character]
- Naomi and Ruth looked for a home where she would be well provided for (3:1) [thinking long-term and taking into account practicalities of real life]
- Ruth came to Boaz in humility and submission (3:4-5) [heart-level focus; inner beauty/character; other-oriented] Ruth put her virtue at risk by going to the threshing floor and lying at Boaz's feet, but she trusted his character and believed he would not take advantage of her.
- Boaz noticed her character again – she did not run after younger men, rich or poor (3:10) and all the townspeople knew her to be of noble character (3:11) [deep, heart-level relationship with the support of a trusted community; focused on inner beauty/character]
- Boaz had thought the situation through and knew there was a closer relative who should have first choice (3:12) [deliberate, thoughtful character; not hurried or impulsive]
- Naomi noticed Boaz's character again – that he was a man of his word (3:18) [focused on inner beauty/character]

4. What questions or concerns do you want to discuss further with us?

Session 4:
Integrity, Self-Control, and Sexual Purity

Session Purpose and Themes

Session Summary:

This session explores practical ways to pursue physical and mental purity. We focus especially on dangers inherent in every type of media as an area of strong and frequent temptation for today's average teen. Even for families purposeful about their exposure to worldly influences, opportunities abound for assault by countless sexual images every day. Temptation is a slippery slope, and the consequences for progressive entrapment by sin, particularly sexual sin, are life-altering. An understanding of God's standards of purity and holiness and a healthy fear of these consequences (and the God who uses them to discipline His children) is one of the greatest gifts you can give your children.

Session Themes:

- God commands that we live a holy and pure life, both with our bodies (physical purity) and our minds (mental purity). We are to offer ourselves, body and mind, as living sacrifices for Christ.
- Although many Christian young people focus primarily on the purity of their bodies, you need to be just as careful to protect the purity of your mind and thoughts. (Matthew 5:28) Particularly for boys, who are more visually oriented, mental purity may be a serious challenge. Once you are exposed to impure sexual images, they can, and often do, stay imbedded in your memory for years, tempting you over and over again to sin in thought or action. (Satan can get a lot of mileage out of "just one picture" or "just this one movie"!)
- It is critical to have a practical strategy for avoiding and overcoming sexual temptation. Like adults, teens need to be armed with Scripture, prayer, both an avoidance and escape plan, and a framework for accountability before they go into battle with the enemy and the world. Sexual purity *is* possible, even in our sex-saturated society, but not without much forethought and preparation.

Hints for a More Effective Study

- Acknowledge that, in today's society, temptation is virtually unavoidable. Temptation is not sin (and we address the difference in this session), but a proactive teen can successfully limit his exposure.
- Emphasize that because sexual temptation is a very slippery slope, even what we might see as a small or inconsequential sin (for example, "locker room talk" or a brief scene in a movie) can start us down a path that easily and naturally leads us deeper into sin (like masturbation, pornography, sexual experimentation, etc.). Because of this, God has clearly defined the radical approach we need to take towards sexual purity in *both* body *and* mind.
- As appropriate, consider whether there are struggles and victories in the area of sexual temptation from your past or present that you feel comfortable sharing with your teen.
- Keep in mind that a primary goal of your discussion should be opening up a continuing dialogue with your teen on these topics. Make sure she understands that there will always be an open door to talk to you about any questions or concerns she might have. Try to create an atmosphere in which she feels comfortable and safe talking to you about such personal and delicate subjects. If she is able to share even struggles and failures with you, you will have the opportunity to help her regain traction on the slippery slope of sexual immorality while she is still easily within reach. You don't want to communicate that you expect her to fail, but you do want her to trust you enough to be real with you.

Precautions

- This session provides the most natural opportunity for a necessary discussion of the topic of masturbation, which is particularly a problem for boys. Our own study of Scripture on this point has led us to conclude that the Bible does not directly address this topic; however, it does offer several principles (such as avoiding lustful thoughts – which almost always accompany masturbation) that make a compelling case for why it should be avoided. You should take some time to study the Bible yourself on this topic before discussing it with your son or daughter.
- The question concerning consequences of sexual impurity in the "Application to Me" section of this session provides a natural opportunity for discussion of sexually transmitted diseases (STD's). Because a desire to avoid consequences is not the primary motivation for Christians in pursuing sexual purity, we have not made the danger of STD's a prominent part of this study; however, this is a very pervasive and devastating problem in today's youth culture and should be addressed with your teen. In the "Additional Resources" section below, we have included reference materials that will help you to educate yourself and your children on the prevalence and serious consequences of STD's.
- In today's sex-saturated society, we believe that it would be difficult to be *too* radical in your approach to sexual purity with your children. Sexual tempation is one of the only tempations we are consistently told in Scripture to "flee"; others we are simply told to "avoid." (See, e.g. 1 Corinthians 6:18; Proverbs 4:14-15; 1 Thessalonians 5:22.) Our society is making an all-out assault on biblical standards. Often its messages are blatant and impossible to miss, but sometimes the message is subtle, disguised, or in an unexpected venue, such as T.V. commercials, magazine covers seen in grocery check-out lines, teen clothing catalogues, etc. We need to challenge our children continually to be proactive, like Joseph with Potiphar's wife, in proactively avoiding and, when necessary, fleeing from any and all situations that would tempt them to sexual sin. This will likely make them stand out from their peers, but gently remind your teen that all disciples of Christ are called to radical obedience – to be in the world, but not of it.
- Even if Satan cannot destroy your child's soul, he will try to destroy his witness. Sexual temptation is a powerful and effective way to destroy a witness for Christ.
- In addition, because of the pervasive influence of sexual immorality in our society, we believe that your child's purity of body and mind is probably one of the most important prayer focuses you should have as parents. We encourage you to pray *faithfully* for the physical, intellectual, spiritual, and emotional purity of your children and their future spouses.

Additional Resources

Arterburn, Stephen and Fred Stoeker with Mike Yorkey. *Every Young Man's Battle: Strategies for Victory in the Real World of Sexual Temptation*. Colorado Springs: Waterbrook Press, 2002. (In particular, we recommend Part IV, "Masturbation," pp. 95-136.) A workbook is also available.

Elliot, Elisabeth. *Passion and Purity: Learning to Bring Your Love Life Under Christ's Control*. Grand Rapids: Fleming H. Revell, 2002.

Elliot, Elisabeth. *Quest for Love: True Stories of Passion and Purity*. Grand Rapids: Fleming H. Revell. 1996.

Ethridge, Shannon and Stephen Arterburn. *Every Young Woman's Battle: Guarding Your Heart, Mind, and Body in a Sex-Saturated World*. Colorado Springs: Random House, Inc., 2004

Harris, Joshua. *Not Even a Hint: Guarding Your Heart Against Lust*. Sisters, Oregon: Multnomah Publishers, 2003. Workbooks are also available for both genders.

"STD Overview." The Medical Institue for Sexual Health. www.medinstitute.org/medical/index.htm.

Part 4A - Parent Discussion Guide

***Introductory comments*:**

- Our sexual drives are real, created by God for a holy purpose (unification, enjoyment and procreation in marriage). They are strong and are both physical and emotional.
- But improper sexual activity is one of the biggest obstacles to godliness today.
- To control these drives in a God-honoring way, we need to rely on God's grace and the work of the Holy Spirit within us.
- We also need a plan to recognize and avoid situations that can get us into temptation. It is not enough just to prepare to fight battles against sexual temptation; we need to work just as hard to avoid exposing ourselves to temptation in the first place. With self-discipline (controlling our own thoughts and behavior with the empowerment of the Holy Spirit), we can consistently demonstrate integrity and make good choices.
- When temptation comes, we have the choice to give in or to resist (turn away), but we need to prepare our hearts and minds in advance if we are to have victory over the wiles of Satan and the pull of our own fleshly desires.
- This session will explore the kinds of temptations you may face, the kind of integrity and purity that God expects of you in all things (particularly sexuality), and some strategies for maintaining your integrity and sexual purity, both before and after you are married.

I. God commands purity/holiness in all aspects of our lives, including how we use our bodies (sexual activity) and our minds (thought life).

A. Holiness:

- God has <u>saved</u> us and <u>called</u> us to a holy life because of His grace. (1 Timothy 1:9)

  1 Timothy 1:9 – "[God] has saved us and called us to a holy life – not because of anything we have done but because of His own purpose and grace."

- God commands us to live <u>holy</u> and <u>godly</u> lives. (1 Peter 3:10-11)

  1 Peter 3:10-11 – "For, 'Whoever would love life and see good days must keep his tongue from evil and his lips from deceitful speech. He must turn from evil and do good; he must seek peace and pursue it.' "

- This includes offering our <u>bodies</u> as living <u>sacrifices</u> – holy and pleasing to God as an act of worship. (Romans 12:1)

  Romans 12:1 – "Therefore, I urge you, brothers, in view of God's mercy, to offer your bodies as living sacrifices, holy and pleasing to God – this is your spiritual act of worship."

- It also involves offering our <u>minds</u> and <u>thoughts</u> to God. (Philippians 4:8)

Philippians 4:8 – "Finally, brothers, whatever is true, whatever is noble, whatever is right, whatever is pure, whatever is lovely, whatever is admirable – if anything is excellent or praiseworthy – think about such things."

B. Purity of Body: Read 1 Corinthians 6: 9-20 and 1 Thessalonians 4:1-8.

What do these verses tell us about our bodies?

- Our bodies were bought at a price – Jesus' suffering and death for our sins. (1 Corinthians 6:20)
- Therefore, our bodies are not our own; they belong to God. (1 Corinthians 6:13, 15)
- They are temples of the Holy Spirit, who lives inside of believers. (1 Corinthians 6:19)
- We should learn to control our own bodies in a way that is holy and honorable to God. (1 Thessalonians 4:4, 7)

What do these verses tell us about God's attitude toward sex and our bodies?

- Sexual sin is a unique sin against your own body. (1 Corinthians 6:18)
- God hates sexual immorality. (1 Corinthians 6:18; 1 Thessalonians 4:3)
- Sexual immorality is a sin and dishonors God. (1 Corinthians 6:18-20)
- We are to flee sexual immorality. (1 Corinthians 6:18)
  - Sexual immorality covers a broad spectrum of sexual behaviors – not just sexual intercourse outside of marriage.
  - Examples of sexual immorality include sensual touch, oral sex, and sexual intercourse outside marriage; masturbation (with lustful thoughts); pornography; lingering looks and sexual fantasizing about someone of the opposite sex; etc.

C. Purity of Mind and Thought: Read Matthew 22:37, Philippians 4:8, and 2 Timothy 2:22.

Matthew 22:37 – "Jesus replied: ' "Love the Lord your God with all your heart and with all your soul and with all your mind." ' "

Philippians 4:8 – "Finally, brothers, whatever is true, whatever is noble, whatever is right, whatever is pure, whatever is lovely, whatever is admirable – if anything is excellent or praiseworthy – think about such things."

2 Timothy 2:22 – "Flee the evil desires of youth, and pursue righteousness, faith, love and peace, along with those who call on the Lord out of a pure heart."

What do these verses tell us that God expects of our minds and thoughts?

- We are to love God with our minds, as well as our hearts. (Matthew 22:37)
- We should focus our minds only on things that are noble, pure, lovely, excellent and praiseworthy. (Philippians 4:8)
- We should flee the evil desires of youth and join others who seek God with a pure heart. (2 Timothy 2:22)

What do each of the following verses tell us about our minds/thought life and sexual sin?

Matthew 5:28 – " 'But I tell you that anyone who looks at a woman lustfully has already committed adultery with her in his heart.' "

❖ We can sin sexually with our <u>minds</u> as well as our bodies.

- Examples: sexual fantasies, viewing pornographic or otherwise inappropriate pictures or videos/movies, reading sexually explicit books, allowing one's glance (and mind) to linger on someone to whom you are sexually attracted, etc.

Ephesians 5:4 – "Nor should there be any obscenity, foolish talk or coarse joking, which are out of place, but rather thanksgiving."

❖ We can sin sexually by engaging in <u>obscenities</u> (sexual words, jokes or comments) or <u>coarse talk</u> (degrading or disrespectful statements about the opposite sex).

- As you go through the teen years, you (guys, especially) will be confronted with many opportunities to engage in sexual jokes and bantering. You will also be tempted to engage in conversations that are disrespectful of the opposite sex.
- This is sinful and should be avoided for many reasons, including:
  - o It starts the mind down a dangerous path toward deeper sin.
  - o It treats the opposite sex like sex objects, not people created in the image of God.
  - o It dishonors the Creator of both sexes and the beauty and holiness of marital love-making.

❖ You may also be tempted to engage in masturbation. (This point is not included in the Student Discussion Notes.)

- As you physically mature (and throughout your adult life), you may have a desire to manually stimulate yourself to a state of orgasm.
- The Bible says nothing about this specifically. (It neither condones nor prohibits it.)
- The danger is that it is almost always accompanied by sexual thoughts and images (fantasies) in your mind.
- Linked with these thoughts, masturbation is dangerous and often sinful. (See Matthew 5:28.) It can also become habit-forming.
- It deprives a spouse (both future and present) of intimacy, because it is a solitary, rather than mutual, sexual experience, which is not what God intended for sexual love. God designed our bodies for mutual sexual pleasure with our spouse. Our spouse is entitled to all of our sexual energy and attention. (See 1 Corinthians 7:4.)
- Finally, habitual masturbation can limit your sexual experiences with your future spouse when you carry many of those thoughts and fantasies into your bedroom when married. Your spouse may not be able to live up to the expectations created by masturbation.
- We want you to come and talk to us anytime you are faced with the urge to masturbate. Temptation is not something to be ashamed of, and this type of temptation is not something you should try to handle on your own. This is one of many areas where we are asking you to be accountable to us as you mature.

Note to parents: Consider sharing, with discretion, your own struggles as a teenager in each of the areas mentioned above.

Read 1 Corinthians 6:18-20 and 1 Timothy 6:11:

1 Corinthians 6:18-20 – "Flee from sexual immorality. All other sins a man commits are outside his body, but he who sins sexually sins against his own body. Do you not know that your body is a temple of the Holy Spirit, who is in you, whom you have received from God? You are not your own; you were bought at a price. Therefore, honor God with your body."

1 Timothy 6:11 – "But you, man of God, flee from all this, and pursue righteousness, godliness, faith, love, endurance and gentleness."

❖ We should flee from all forms of worldly temptations, including sexual immorality, and instead honor God with our bodies by pursuing a life of godly love and purity.

WARNING: You need to be as careful about your purity of mind as you are about your purity of body. Once you (particularly guys) are exposed to impure sexual images (pictures, movie scenes, etc.), they are likely to stay in your memory for a long time and will come back time and time again, tempting you to sin (in action and in thought).

D. Application to Me

1. What types of things or situations in your life bring images, thoughts, or opportunities that could drive your sexual desires toward immorality?

   Answers will vary but could include:
   - Television shows and commercials (including commercials during shows considered morally acceptable or neutral, like sporting events)
   - Movie scenes (including trailers for upcoming movies shown before movies you might consider safe)
   - Internet sites
   - Pornographic magazines (e.g. *Playboy*, *Penthouse, Playgirl*) and other magazines not categorized by the world as "pornographic" but which feature covers, photo shoots, and articles that are inappropriate and sexual in nature (e.g. *Cosmopolitan*)
   - Lingerie Catalogs
   - Sporting and automobile magazines (e.g. *Sports Illustrated* – ads and pictures, in addition to the annual "swimsuit issue")
   - Billboards
   - Sexually explicit lyrics in songs and images in music videos
   - Romance novels
   - Lingering glances
   - Friends with loose moral standards
   - Peers dressed immodestly (intentionally and unintentionally)
   - Sexually-based teasing, bantering, or jokes

2. The Bible tells us to "guard our hearts and minds" (Philippians 4:7) and "flee from sexual immorality." (1 Corinthians 6:18) What kinds of strategies can you use to guard your heart and mind from the sexual temptation that is all around us?

   Answers will vary but might include:
   - Put on the full armor of God. (Ephesians 6:10-18)
   - **FLEE** anything that could be a sexual temptation. "Submit yourselves, then, to God. Resist the devil, and he will flee from you." (James 4:7)
   - Think about and focus on what is pure and right. Fill your mind with music, books, and images that elevate your thought life.
   - Memorize Scripture and meditate on it as you go through your day, particularly when tempted by an impure thought.
   - Watch very little, if any, T.V. Tape carefully selected shows and/or sporting events that your family decides are edifying, instead of watching them at the time they are originally broadcast so that you can edit commercials, half-time shows, etc. Watch T.V. as a family or with at least one parent, rather than on your own. If you choose to watch a program "live," as opposed to taping it first, turn off or mute commercials. (Be aware, however, that T.V. commercials are visually offensive, as well, so it may be better simply to leave the room during the ads.) Some families might decide that choosing to watch any television is like deciding if you want a lot, or just a little, sewage in your mind!
   - Screen movies and videos carefully. (Use websites such as www.screenit.com and magazines such as *Plugged In* to help you make wise choices *before* you enter the theater.) Be extremely selective about what you allow your eyes to see and your ears to hear, no matter what the rating is or what other Christian kids are seeing. Also, be careful about previews for upcoming movies that are shown in theaters before a feature film. Know what your particular temptations are: If you know that hearing swearing causes you to think and/or say those words yourself, you will need to be more careful about exposure to that than a friend or sibling may need to be. Parents, set an example in your own viewing. Develop habits that you would want your teen to imitate. **Remember that once you have seen or heard something inappropriate, it is likely to be stored in your mind forever.**
   - Monitor your internet usage. Use a service such as www.covenanteyes.com to have a monthly internet report sent to someone else for accountability regarding the sites you visit.
   - Choose carefully which magazines you read or even pick up to browse at the doctor's office or in the check-out line at the grocery store. Guys, have Mom preview your sports and car magazines and rip out inappropriate ads and/or articles before you see them.
   - Pursue accountability with your parents, a trusted friend, or a discipleship group.

3. What is the difference between temptation and sin? What is the best way to respond to temptation?

   Note to parents: It is essential that you help your child understand the distinction between temptation and sin so that she is not tormented by false guilt for thoughts over which she has no control.
   - Temptation is the initial thought that Satan and our own sinful nature use to entice us to sin. (See James 1:14.)
   - Sin is choosing to dwell on, linger over, pursue, or act on that temptation.

- Between temptation and sin is **choice**. With the empowering of the Holy Spirit, we are equipped to resist temptation and to escape sin before its first tentacles capture us. The longer we wait to turn from temptation, the harder it is to escape sin's power and the greater the consequences we will suffer for our sin.
- In 1 Corinthians 10:13 God tells us that we won't be tempted beyond what we can bear and that He will provide a way of escape. When tempted, *look* for the "way of escape" - it is *always* there!

4. What are some consequences that could occur when someone engages in sexual activities outside of marriage?

Answers will vary but may include:

- Pregnancy and sexually transmitted diseases (including AIDS, gonorrhea, syphilis)
- Guilt and shame for your sin and for letting down God, yourself, your family, your friends, and anyone looking to you as a window to Christ
- Memories of prior relationships that will stay with you forever and will likely haunt your marriage, which robs you and your spouse of the opportunity to explore the gift of sexual love freely for the first time with one another
- Hurt and loss of trust for your spouse and children and potential divorce if your sexual sin takes place or continues after you are married (adultery)
- The creation of a physical, emotional, and spiritual bond with someone other than your spouse
- A damaged (though not irredeemable) witness for Christ
- Inability to present yourself to your future spouse as a sexual gift *totally* reserved for him or her
- Eventual resentment(in wives) and disrespect (in husbands) if you eventually marry the person with whom you sinned
- Alienation from God until you repent
- Greater difficulty resisting future temptation
- Greater potential for lowering moral standards in other areas of your life
- Emotional scars that may never heal from participating in things that a youth is not emotionally ready to experiance

Conclusion: God commands that we live holy and pure lives in both our bodies and our minds. Our best strategy is to identify, avoid, and FLEE any form of temptation to sexual immorality and diligently pursue godly love and purity in all areas of life.

Part 4B - Student Discussion Notes

I. God commands purity/holiness in all aspects of our lives, including how we use our bodies (sexual activity) and our minds (thought life).

A. Holiness:

- God has ____________ us and _____________ us to a holy life because of His grace. (2 Timothy 1:9)
- God commands us to live ___________ and ___________ lives. (1 Peter 3:10-11)
- This includes offering our __________ as living _____________ – holy and pleasing to God as an act of worship. (Romans 12:1)
- It also involves offering our __________ and ____________ to God. (Philippians 4:8)

B. Purity of Body: Read 1 Corinthians 6: 9-20 and 1 Thessalonians 4:1-8.

What do these verses tell us about our bodies?

- Our bodies were bought at a ____________ – Jesus' suffering and death for our sins. (1 Corinthians 6:20)
- Therefore, our bodies are not our own; they belong to __________. (1 Corinthians 6:13, 15)
- They are _____________ of the Holy Spirit, who lives inside of believers. (1 Corinthians 6: 19)
- We should learn to ____________ our own bodies in a way that is holy and ____________ to God. (1 Thessalonians 4:4, 7)

What do these verses tell us about God's attitude toward sex and our bodies?

- Sexual sin is a unique sin against your own ______________. (1 Corinthians 6:18)
- God hates __________ ______________. (1 Corinthians 6:18; 1 Thessalonians 4:3)
- Sexual immorality is a ___________ and dishonors God. (1 Corinthians 6:18-20)
- We are to _________ sexual immorality. (1 Corinthians 6:18)

C. Purity of Mind and Thought: Read Matthew 22:37, Philippians 4:8, and 2 Timothy 2:22.

What do these verses tell us that God expects of our minds and thoughts?

- ❖ We are to love God with our ____________, as well as our hearts. (Matthew 22:37)
- ❖ We should focus our minds only on things that are noble, _______, lovely, excellent and praiseworthy. (Philippians 4:8)
- ❖ We should ________ the evil desires of youth and _______ others who seek God with a pure heart. (2 Timothy 2:22)

What do each of the following verses tell us about our minds/thought life and sexual sin?

- ❖ We can sin sexually with our __________, as well as our bodies. (Matthew 5:28)
- ❖ We can sin sexually by engaging in _____________ (sexual words, jokes or comments) or ___________ _________ (degrading or disrespectful statements about the opposite sex). (Ephesians 5:4)
- ❖ We should ____________ from all forms of worldly temptations, including sexual immorality, and instead, honor God with our bodies by _______________ a life of godly love and purity. (1 Corinthians 6:18-20; 1 Timothy 6:11)

WARNING: You need to be as careful about your purity of mind as you are about your purity of body. Once you (guys particularly) are exposed to impure sexual images (pictures, movie scenes, etc.), they are likely to stay in your memory for a long time and will come back time and time again, tempting you to sin (in action and in thought).

D. Application to Me

1. What types of things or situations in your life bring images, thoughts, or opportunities that could drive your sexual desires toward immorality?

2. The Bible tells us to "guard our hearts and minds" (Philippians 4:7) and "flee from sexual immorality." (1 Corinthians 6:18) What kinds of strategies can you use to guard your heart and mind from the sexual temptation that is all around us?

3. What is the difference between temptation and sin? What is the best way to respond to temptation?

4. What are some consequences that could occur when someone engages in sexual activities outside of marriage?

Conclusion: God commands that we live holy and pure lives in both our bodies and our minds. Our best strategy is to identify, avoid, and FLEE any form of temptation to sexual immorality and diligently pursue godly love and purity in all areas of life.

Part 4C - Student Follow-up Study

1. The story of King Solomon and his many wives is a good example of not dealing effectively and successfully with sexual temptation. (1 Kings 11:1-13) Read the story and then list the temptations to which Solomon succumbed and the consequences of his failure to resist those temptations.

2. The story of Joseph and Potiphar's wife (Genesis 39:1-12) is a good example of dealing effectively and successfully with sexual temptation. Read the story and then list both the nature of the temptations Potiphar's wife offered Joseph and his strategy for dealing with them.

3. From our study together, what have you learned about why purity of mind and body is important before marriage?

4. How can you protect your purity of mind and body now as you grow through the teen years? (Make a list of specific ways.)

5. How can we as your parents pray for these things for you today?

6. One effective way to flee temptation is to memorize Scripture that will remind you of what God desires of you and how He empowers you to experience victory over sin. Before our next session, choose and memorize at least one Scripture verse that will help you deal with these temptations when they come. Below are some verses on this topic from which you might want to choose. You should choose a verse that is most meaningful to you. (It does not have to come from this list.)

1 Corinthians 6:18-20	Philippians 4:8	Matthew 22:37
1 Timothy 6:11	2 Timothy 2:22	Romans 12:1
Colossians 1:10-12	2 Timothy 1:7	1 Corinthians 10:13
1 Corinthians 15:56-57	Philippians 4:13	1 John 5:4-5

7. What questions or concerns do you want to discuss further with us?

Part 4D - Parent Follow-up Guide

1. **The story of King Solomon and his many wives is a good example of not dealing effectively and successfully with sexual temptation. (1 Kings 11:1-13) Read the story and then list the temptations to which Solomon succumbed and the consequences of his failure to resist those temptations.**

   - Solomon pursued many foreign wives to whom he "held fast . . . in love." (11:2)
   - He had multiple wives and concubines (700 wives of royal birth and 300 concubines). (11:3)
   - His wives led him astray (11:3) and turned his heart toward other gods, so that his heart was not fully devoted to God. (11:4-6) He built altars for his foreign wives. (11:7-8)
   - God became angry with him and told him that his kingdom would be taken away from him (although not until the reign of his son). (11:9-13)

2. **The story of Joseph and Potiphar's wife (Genesis 39:1-12) is a good example of dealing effectively and successfully with sexual temptation. Read the story and then list both the nature of the temptations Potiphar's wife offered Joseph and his strategy for dealing with them.**

   - The temptations confronted Joseph on an almost daily basis (39:7-10) – not unlike what young people face in our world today. Joseph had to refuse the advances of Potiphar's wife continually (persistence).
   - Joseph refused her and offered her reasons why he was doing so (resistance). (39:8-9)
   - He refused even to be with her (avoidance). (39:10)
   - He immediately ran away when she forced herself on him (flight). (39:12)
   - Our culture insists that it is impossible to overcome sexual temptation, so we are told we should simply do our best to minimize the risks associated with sex outside of marriage. Males, in particular, are led to believe that they are incapable of resisting their natural desires and that if anyone is to keep sexual sin from occurring, it is the female who must set the standard and "just say no." This is *not* biblical.
   - Joseph's example, however, demonstrates that it is possible for all of us – males and females – to overcome temptation, no matter how strong, frequent, and attractive that temptation may be. Notice his strategy: **persistence, resistance, avoidance** and, ultimately, **flight**.

   NOTE: Joseph suffered for his faithfulness but was eventually rewarded by God for his obedience in difficult circumstances. (See Genesis 41:39-45.)

3. **From our study together, what have you learned about why purity of mind and body is important before marriage?**

   Answers will vary but may include:
   - It pleases God and glorifies Him.
   - It protects the gift of sexual love for you and your future spouse to discover and explore together.
   - Participating in any kind of sexual behavior before marriage will leave you with memories and experiences that you will carry into your sexual relationship with your spouse.

- Exposure to pornography and sexually explicit videos and movies will also leave you with pictures/images in your mind and unrealistic expectations about sexual love that could cause you to be disappointed with what you actually experience and lead to marital problems.
- Sexual promiscuity (even sexual experimentation with just one person, just one time) can result in pregnancy and/or diseases which could plague you and your future spouse for the rest of your life.

4. **How can you protect your purity of mind and body now as you grow through the teen years? (Make a list of specific ways.)**

   Note to parents: Take this opportunity to strategize with your teen how to avoid and flee temptation. Be as practical and creative as possible.

   Answers will vary but may include:
   - FLEE anything that could be a sexual temptation.
   - Acknowledge my areas of greatest weakness and strategize to avoid temptation in these areas in particular.
   - Remember that just because I am a Christian, my date or betrothed is a Christian, or we are both Christians, does not mean we are immune. **Don't let your guard down!**
   - Develop a moral "grid" through which to evaluate what I read, view, and hear.
   - Seek accountability.
   - Fill my mind and occupy my body with things which glorify God and have eternal value.
   - Pray! Ask others to pray for me specifically in this area.

5. **How can we as your parents pray for these things for you today?**
   Answers will vary but may include:
   - Pray that I will be protected from unnecessary temptation and that, when tempted, I will remain faithful to my commitment to purity.
   - Pray that I will be candid and honest in my accountability relationships with you and others. Pray for my humility – that I would seek help when I need it.
   - Pray that my relationship with God will continue to strengthen and mature.
   - Pray for both the purity of my future spouse and for his or her parents as they train and protect him or her.

6. **One effective way to flee temptation is to memorize Scripture that will remind you of what God desires of you and how He empowers you to experience victory over sin. Before our next session, choose and memorize at least one Scripture verse that will help you deal with these temptations when they come. Below are some verses on this topic from which you might want to choose. You should choose a verse that is most meaningful to you. (It does not have to come from this list.)**

   1 Corinthians 6:18-20
   1 Timothy 6:11
   Colossians 1:10-12
   1 Corinthians 15:56-57
   Philippians 4:8
   2 Timothy 2:22
   2 Timothy 1:7
   Philippians 4:13
   Matthew 22:37
   Romans 12:1
   1 Corinthians 10:13
   1 John 5:4-5

7. **What questions or concerns do you want to discuss further with us?**

Session 5: Whom and When Should I Date?

Session Purpose and Themes

Session Summary:

- This lesson addresses the topic of dating: What does the Bible say about it (either directly or through general biblical principles)? Should Christian teens date? If so, who should they date? Are there alternatives to dating? This is currently a hot topic in Christian circles, with some families rejecting dating completely (and employing some form of traditional courtship for their children) and others attempting to structure dating so that, with the enabling of the Holy Spirit, purity of emotions and body can be maintained.
- We cannot answer the dating question for you and your teen. We do not believe that the Bible specifically prohibits or endorses dating (although the Follow-Up Study for this session does introduce examples from Scripture of both successful and unsuccessful approaches to finding a spouse). If you have not already established a family approach to dating, you will need to take some time to consider the options available. (We discuss this more fully below in "Hints for a More Effective Study.") We have chosen to present our own conclusions and leave it to you to decide how to use this session with your children. The important point is to reach a deliberate decision on the matter as opposed to simply ending up with one approach or the other by default.

Session Themes:

- o God does not want us to develop (be "yoked" in) intimate relationships such as dating and marriage with non-Christians.
- o While the Bible neither endorses nor prohibits dating as practiced by our culture, we (Jeff and Pam) have come to the conclusion that recreational dating is generally not effective in helping to prepare young people for a committed, lasting relationship with a "suitable" spouse. In fact, it very often places teens in dangerous situations fraught with temptation.
- o Throughout the teen years our children can focus on pursuing "NOBLE" friendships (explained in the lesson), developing their own character, and observing a variety of people in diverse situations those character qualities that will someday make someone a "suitable" spouse for them.

Hints for a More Effective Study

- "NOBLE" is an acronym we developed to help our children think about desirable character qualities for which to look in close friends. If you have done something similar with your own children, you could use that instead. Or consider undertaking a project with your whole family (siblings included) to create your own family's guidelines for choosing friends. (This might make a fun, interactive family devotion.)
- A new or different approach to dating might be a volatile topic with your teen. If you have not already done so, we recommend that you spend considerable time as a couple studying, discussing, and praying about the approach God would have you take on this subject with your children. Consider reading some or all of the resources we list below to get a full and balanced perspective on dating and some suggested alternatives. Consider questions such as: Do we believe our children should date at all during the teen years? If so, what kind of dating is acceptable (e.g., group dates or occasional dates for special events like homecoming or prom, long-term relationships with one person, or "playing the field" without serious emotional attachments)? If dating is not advisable, how will we redirect our children's

interests during this stage of life? Parents, in agreement, should review and tailor the summary portion of the student outline to reflect the conclusions that you want to convey to *your* children.

- We have tried to structure a carefully balanced approach to the topic. This involves looking at dating from many angles, which is the primary reason why Session 5 is the longest of the six studies. We begin by asking what the benefits of dating might be and why our children might want to date. This gives them the opportunity, if they wish, to articulate the strongest case they can in favor of it. We then lead them through a discussion of the principal limitations and dangers we believe are inherent in recreational dating during the teen years. Our goal with our own children is to help them make well-informed decisions in this area well BEFORE they reach traditional dating age with expectations already formed by the world. In a best-case scenario our children would, after considering all the facts and principles involved, and knowing both the potential benefits and the potential dangers, make a decision for themselves that serious dating is not a wise investment of time and emotions at this stage in their lives. We designed the lesson to help them arrive at this conclusion. Again, this was our desire for *our* family.
- This is a topic that you should consistently revisit as a couple and with your teen. As your children move further into the teen years, we urge you to consider reading some books on this topic together, such as the resources we have listed below. These should encourage your teen and reveal to him that he is not alone in stepping off the path the rest of the world is taking. Your additional reading may confirm your current approach to dating or challenge you to reconsider it. Most importantly, it will keep you and your teen talking about this topic and encourage open dialogue, which will be particularly important if you and your teen are not presently on the same page about dating.
- Continue to brainstorm after this session and encourage your teen to come to you with any questions he has about the guidelines you have set up together, particularly as new, unanticipated situations arise.
- We suggest you begin by discussing how you will handle mixed large-group activities, special events where dates are traditional (like school dances or family weddings), group dates, double dates, blind dates, getting a ride from someone of the opposite sex, asking a friend of the opposite sex over to your home, making and accepting phone calls from the opposite sex, etc. You will not be able to anticipate every situation, nor do you want to become legalistic, but the more prepared both you and your teen are before potential challenges arise, the better. It creates much less stress in the long-run if decisions don't have to be made ad-hoc and in the heat of the moment. There will be less conflict and debate each time situations arise if you and your teen know what to expect in advance.
- You will also need to address group situations which, although not dates *per se*, commonly result in couplings. Teens today often do not go on traditional "dates," but it is well known by their peers that they are a couple. This occurs in youth groups as commonly as in schools. If your family decision is to defer dating, you and your teen should discuss ways for him to avoid developing the kind of exclusive friendships that often lead to "unofficial" dating.
- We believe it is important, particularly if your teen chooses not to date or to leave serious dating for a later stage in life, that you help her develop a humble answer to the questions she will inevitably receive about her decision from both peers and adults. (In *I Kissed Dating Goodb*ye, Joshua Harris gives some excellent suggestions for the manner in which a teen could effectively express an untraditional position on dating. See "Additional Resources" below.) Once developed, your teen's response could be practiced with you so that she is prepared with a confident, clear, and humble explanation of your family's dating philosophy (in her words, not yours). Make sure you encourage your teen to spend considerable time on Questions 3 and 4 in the Student Follow-Up Study, which address these two important questions.
- Spend some time studying and discussing the four Bible stories in the Student Follow Up Study. These stories (two with positive outcomes and two with negative) are surprisingly relevant to the topic of dating in today's culture and provide a wonderful backdrop for a follow-up discussion about this topic.

- It would be wise for you and your teen to put your general philosophy and some specific guidelines on paper to avoid future confusion. You should consider having both you and your teen sign the document to indicate that you all commit to the standards established.
- This may be a very malleable agreement if you have determined you will reconsider and potentially change the guidelines as your teen reaches new levels of maturity; we suggest, however, that part of your original agreement be that no changes will be made without "due process" – forethought, discussion, prayer, and agreement. (This means that your teen agrees not to run in on Friday afternoon with a request to go out that same night in a manner that has not been addressed by, or would require a change in, the current agreement.)
- Parents should always have the final authority if an impasse is reached or if the current guidelines aren't working.

Precautions

- Our primary precaution has already been stated: Because of the absence of definitive biblical standards in this area, our discussion of dating in this session is based on our personal conviction that serious dating (an exclusive, long-term, intimate relationship with someone of the opposite sex) during the teen years is in most cases not a wise or productive use of time (for a variety of reasons which we discuss in the session). These are issues about which you, as a couple, should come to agreement before you broach the topic with your teen.
- In our discussion of Paul's caution not to be unequally "yoked" with unbelievers in 2 Corinthians 6:14-15, we are not suggesting that Christians, including our teenage children, should isolate themselves from the secular world or their unsaved friends. While our children, even as teens, are still in training and not yet spiritually mature, God does offer them opportunities, as believers, to engage the world as "salt and light" (Matthew 5:13-16) with the goal of spreading the gospel of Christ in their spheres of influence. But it is essential that they avoid developing deeper, more intimate relationships (such as marriage or serious dating relationships) with non-Christians for reasons we discuss in the lesson.

Additional Resources

Cloud, Henry and John Townsend. *Boundaries in Dating: Making Dating Work.* Grand Rapids: Zondervan Publishing House, 2000.

Eliot, Elisabeth. *Passion and Purity: Learning to Bring Your Love Life Under Christ's Control.* Grand Rapids: F.H. Revell, 2002.

Harris, Joshua. *Boy Meets Girl: Say Hello to Courtship.* Sisters, Oregon: Multnomah Books, 2000.

Harris, Joshua. *I Kissed Dating Goodbye: A New Attitude Toward Romance and Relationships.* Sisters, Oregon: Multnomah Books, 1997.

McDowell, Josh. *Why Wait?: What You Need to Know About the Teen Sexuality Crisis.* San Bernardino: Here's Life Publishers, 1987.

Myers, Jeff and Danielle. *Of Knights and Fair Maidens: A Radical New Way to Develop Old-Fashioned Relationships.* Johnson City, TN : Appalacian Distributors, 2003.

Part 5A - Parent Discussion Guide

***Introductory comments*:**

- Today, people view dating as a primary vehicle for guys and girls to learn about the opposite sex, have fun with one another, and relate to one another. Eventually, it is believed, dating will help a young person to discover and then get to know the person he or she will eventually marry.
- Dating as most of western culture engages in it today has not always, however, been the preferred approach to accomplishing these important goals, and recently a small but growing number of Christian families in America have begun to propose alternatives to what we call "recreational dating."
- In this study, we will begin to explore what the Bible has to say about the people with whom we should have intimate relationships, some characteristics for which we should look in close friends, and how well dating does or does not help us find a "suitable" person to marry.

I. Equally Yoked: God's Design for Intimate Relationships

Read 2 Corinthians 6:14-15 and Deuteronomy 22:10. What does it mean to be "yoked" together?

❖ Being "yoked" together means to be joined in a relatively permanent or serious way for the purpose of accomplishing some goal or objective.
  - The Deuteronomy passage tells the Israelites not to "yoke" an ox and a donkey together (presumably for plowing purposes) because their different gaits and temperaments make it difficult for them to work together effectively.

What does this passage suggest our attitude and approach to close and intimate relationships (like dating and marriage) with the opposite sex should be?

- The passage tells us that we should not be "yoked" together with unbelievers. It uses words like "have in common," "fellowship," and "harmony," indicating that the relationships at issue are not just casual acquaintances but close and intimate relationships.

❖ It suggests that we should not marry (or potentially even date) someone who is not a believer.

Why would God want us to have intimate relationships (like close friendship and marriage) only with believers? Think about the implications of the passages above and read 1 Cor. 15:33 and Psalm 1.

❖ We cannot associate regularly and closely with others without "rubbing off" on one another.
  - When we are in close fellowship with strong believers, we improve one another. (Prov. 27:17)
  - When we are in close fellowship with unbelievers, we may influence them for good, but they may also influence us for evil. (See Proverbs 22:24-25; 1 Corinthians 15:33.)

❖ The more time we spend and the more intimacy we create with an unbeliever, the stronger the temptation will be to join him in sin.
  - One example of this is Solomon and his many wives in 1 Kings 11.
  - Notice the progression of intimacy in Psalm 1 from walking (keeping pace with), to standing (identifying with), to sitting (making oneself at home with) the sinner. Those who choose to abide with sinners forfeit God's greatest blessings. (Psalm 1:3,6)

❖ Because Christ must be the center of any vibrant and fulfilling Christian marriage, marrying an unbeliever will necessarily limit the <u>health</u> and <u>intimacy</u> of your marriage and limit your <u>witness</u> as a couple and a family.
  - It can also lead to dangerous conflicts over a variety of issues and decisions (like how to spend money, what to teach your children about God, whether your family should attend church, etc.) because of the difference in moral values and standards between the two of you.

❖ A spiritual bond with a non-Christian <u>weakens</u> our bond with Christ.
  - We cannot be friends with God and friends with a sinful world. (See James 4:4-5.)
  - We cannot participate in the light if we live in darkness. (See 1 John 1:5-7.)

Read Matthew 5: 13-16. How does God want us to relate to unbelievers?

❖ We are to be "<u>salt</u> and <u>light</u>" in order to redeem for Christ those in our circle of influence.
  - We are to be salt in the sense that we are different from the world in our actions and attitudes; this gives us a different flavor, which attracts those who are seeking God.
  - We are light in the sense that we profess and live by the clear and absolute moral standards in God's Word that shine His love and truth into the darkness of the world around us.
  - While being salt and light requires interacting regularly with the unsaved, we must at the same time ultimately remain separate; we are not to be "yoked" with them (to become one with them) for any reason, even in an attempt to win them to Christ.

II. Friendship and Dating

A. Friendship

If God does not want us to be unequally yoked with unbelievers, what does that mean for the kinds of close friends we should make?

❖ We should choose to have *close* friendships primarily, if not exclusively, with other like-minded <u>Christians</u>.
  - Because fellow believers share our faith and values, they will be a good influence on us – and we on them – as we grow and mature. This is particularly vital in the teen years, when peer influence is so strong.
  - See 1 Samuel 19-20 for a window into the healthy intimacy between David and Jonathan. Even in the face of strong opposition, Jonathan shared David's values and remained committed to protecting his friend and advancing God's kingdom at great personal cost. This is an excellent model for our teens.

What are the characteristics of a godly friend?

- After discussing the following acrostic, you may wish to use it as a standard by which to help your teen evaluate her present friendships and develop future friendships that honor God, or you may wish to develop your own family philosophy of friendship. We encourage you to put it in writing so that your teen will have an objective standard upon which to base the friendship choices she makes as she moves through the peer challenges of the teen years.

N<u>ever</u> draw the other into sin. (1 Peter 1:14-16)

> "As obedient children, do not conform to the evil desires you had when you lived in ignorance. But just as He who called you is holy, so be holy in all you do; for it is written: 'Be holy, because I am holy.'"

O<u>ppose</u> the world's ways. (Romans 12:2; Ephesians 4:22-24)

> "Do not conform any longer to the pattern of this world, but be transformed by the renewing of your mind. Then you will be able to test and approve what God's will is – His good, pleasing and perfect will." (Romans 12:2)

> "You were taught, with regard to your former way of life, to put off your old self, which is being corrupted by its deceitful desires; to be made new in the attitude of your minds; and to put on the new self, created to be like God in true righteousness and holiness." (Ephesians 4:22-24)

B<u>uild</u> each other up. (Ephesians 4:29)

> "Do not let any unwholesome talk come out of your mouths, but only what is helpful for building others up according to their needs, that it may benefit those who listen."

L<u>ook</u> for what is best in the other, their family, and all things. (Philippians 4:8)

> "Finally, brothers, whatever is true, whatever is noble, whatever is right, whatever is pure, whatever is lovely, whatever is admirable – if anything is excellent or praiseworthy – think about such things."

E<u>ncourage</u> each other to do the right, loving, and selfless thing. (Hebrews 10:24)

> "And let us consider how we may spur one another on toward love and good deeds."

Where would you begin to look for godly friends? Why?

Answers will vary but may include:

- Youth group/church (because people there are likely to share my faith)
- Family friends – e.g. children of parents' friends (because we probably have a lot, including faith and moral values, in common)
- Camps/retreats (because people there are likely to share my faith)
- Community service/mission projects (because the desire to serve others is one indicator of a person of "NOBLE" character)
- School (because I spend a lot of time there)
- Neighborhood (because they are conveniently located and it is easy to spend time with them)
- Sports teams (because we have a common interest)
- Family - both immediate and extended

Note to parents: Discuss how some of the above have greater potential than others as places to look for godly friends, but note that we might be surprised, too, at how God brings a "NOBLE" friend across our path!

B. Dating

Define "dating." What are its purposes and/or goals?

- In our culture, dating is generally viewed as a casual, recreational activity through which people learn about the opposite sex, seek to have emotional needs met, and often experiment sexually.
- *Webster's Dictionary* defines a date as a social engagement with a member of the opposite sex. It has also come to describe the setting apart of two people of the opposite sex as a couple (e.g. "Tom and Sue are dating").

What do you think might be some benefits of dating?

Answers will vary but may include:

- Dating provides a way to learn about the opposite sex – how they think and communicate, what drives and motivates them, and how to relate to them effectively. This better prepares someone for making a long-term marriage commitment to the "right" person.
- Dating gives people the chance to discover what they like and don't like in the opposite sex (physical characteristics, temperament, family background, communication style, etc.), so that they are better prepared to choose a life partner when that time comes.
- Dating provides opportunities to develop intimacy with a member of the opposite sex, which meets emotional needs and introduces one to the closeness that is consummated in marriage.
- Dating is fun! It is a way to get out and do things with people one's own age and to be part of the social scene at school, at church, and/or in the community.

What do you think may be some drawbacks to dating?

Answers will vary. The rest of this session will highlight many drawbacks, but others include:

- In and of itself, of course, dating (having a social engagement with a member of the opposite sex and/or setting oneself apart with someone else as a couple) is not sinful. But conventional dating can often *lead* to sin, because it places people in situations – both physical and emotional – which pose strong temptations to people of both sexes. (Remember what we learned in Session 4 about the wisdom of avoiding temptation, rather than flirting with it.)
- Recreational dating actually prepares you as much for divorce as for marriage, because a series of broken, short-term relationships does not prepare you for the long-term commitment of marriage.
- People often do not gain the benefits they expect from dating. The purposes of dating mentioned above are rarely fulfilled by conventional dating. In the next section of this lesson, we will review some of the reasons for this.
- Dating usually excludes, or at least partially supplants, parental guidence in mate selection. It can severely limit a parent's positive contribution.

Dating Dangers[1]

As exciting and enticing as dating may seem on the surface, it is generally not all that helpful or effective in helping to find the person who is "suitable" for you as a spouse. Let's look at some of the ways that dating can actually be counterproductive toward these ends.

1. Adapted from Joshua Harris's *I Kissed Dating Goodbye: A New Attitude Toward Romance and Relationships* (Sisters, Oregon: Multinomah Books).

1. Dating creates an <u>artificial</u> environment for evaluating <u>character</u>.
   - Part of the reason dating is fun is that it is a break from real life. When considering a potential mate, we need answers to questions dating isn't designed to (and probably won't) answer.
   - The qualities that make a good boyfriend or girlfriend, particularly when you are young, are not the same qualities that make a good husband or wife; therefore, the argument that dating enables teens to discover qualities in the opposite sex that they would like to look for in a future spouse is rarely valid.
   - If one is looking for a spouse, recreational dating does not offer many opportunities to observe a person's true strengths and weaknesses. It is much more useful to see someone interacting with his family, reacting to stress, and living out his faith in a natural environment than to see him in the idealized environment of a traditional "date."

2. Dating tends to skip the <u>friendship</u> stage of relationships.
   - The premise of dating is: "We're attracted to each other; let's get to know each other." The premise of friendship is: "We have a lot in common; let's enjoy our common interests together."
   - Ideally, friendship should come before dating so that the relationship can ripen at a healthy pace.
   - Friendship gives a relationship between the opposite sexes a firm foundation on which to build a romantic relationship, should that be desired. A strong foundation of friendship gives a couple staying power for those seasons in a relationship when physical attraction alone is not enough to ensure a continuing commitment.

3. Dating often mistakes a <u>physical</u> relationship for <u>love</u>.
   - Dating frequently creates feelings of closeness which are superficial and premature.
   - When physical attraction is the primary focus of a relationship, it becomes difficult to maintain one's objectivity. The physical pleasure being experienced and the illusion of emotional closeness this creates can make infatuation and lust *feel* like love; however, true love, as we have already discussed, is much more than a feeling (and certainly more than physical chemistry).
   - The focus of dating is typically on the present and the self, instead of the future (including eternity) and the other person. Often, what we perceive as love for another person is actually a love for how that person makes us feel about ourselves.
   - Remember that you carry lasting emotional bonds and memories of past physical involvement with others into marriage, which robs you and your future spouse of priceless, exclusive experiences.

4. Dating leads to <u>intimacy</u>, but not necessarily to <u>commitment</u>.
   - Most often dating is short-term and experimental. Thus, a dating couple will commonly develop intimacy on physical and emotional levels (usually much too quickly) without the corresponding level of commitment required to make this intimacy meaningful and long-lasting.

5. Dating often <u>isolates</u> a couple from other vital <u>relationships</u>.
   - When you set yourself apart with one other person as a dating couple, you often miss opportunities for involvement with family, friends, and ministry.

- Over time, the exclusivity of dating can take a toll on other relationships. Although a couple may not intend to isolate themselves, their desire for physical and emotional intimacy often leads them to spend more and more time alone with one another. This is unwise, particularly in the teen years, when the influence of family, mentors, and other godly people in a wide variety of roles is vital to a teen's maturation. Isolation also exponentially increases opportunities to give in to sexual temptation without the safeguards that community provides.

6. Dating, in many cases, distracts young adults from their primary responsibility of preparing for the future.
   - Dating frequently wastes time and energy on a relationship that likely will not last, particularly if those dating are still in their teen years, when it is usually too early to consider marriage.
   - Dating also unnecessarily consumes emotional energy and spiritual resources in a constant battle against sexual temptation that could be better spent elsewhere. The threshold of physical intimacy commonly is pushed back every time a teen enters into a new romantic relationship. (Instead of starting at the beginning of a natural progression of physical intimacy, teens tend to start with a new partner where they left off with the last.) And the longer a couple remains in a relationship, the greater the temptation to seek deeper levels of physical intimacy. As time goes on, it takes progressively more physical intimacy to meet desire. Obviously, this is dangerous.
   - A Christian teen's time would be better spent in a variety of other arenas, which will be discussed in greater detail later in this session.

7. Dating can cause discontentment with God's gift of singleness.
   - The freedom of singleness is a unique opportunity to serve God!
   - Dating gives singles just enough of a taste of intimacy to make them desire more. Desiring what God does not have in store for us *yet* can significantly impair our ability to enjoy and appreciate what He has available for us *now*.

III. Application to Me

What will my approach to dating be?

Answers will vary depending on your family's dating philosophy.

- In rare cases, individuals are ready for marriage in their teen years; however, in today's world, where life is more and more complex and life skills take longer to acquire, this is the exception, rather than the rule.
- Yes, dating is attractive: Everyone else is doing it; it makes you feel good about yourself to know someone finds you special; you desire physical and emotional intimacy; and it is fun to have someone of the opposite sex to do things with. But, for many reasons, it just doesn't make sense at this time in your life.
- You are young and have many years ahead of you to seek and meet a life partner. The people you would get to know through dating today are, like you, still changing, maturing, and developing, so people you get to know today are very different from what they will be when you and they are mature adults and ready for marriage. In addition, you are not well-equipped to assess accurately your own or the other person's level of spiritual maturity at this age.

- Each season of life yields its own unique treasures and builds on the season before it. Our attempts to rush God's timing can spoil the fruit of our lives. Just because something is good doesn't mean we should pursue it right now.
- If you were to develop an intimate relationship at this age, with years to go before you could get married, you would very likely face intense sexual pressure and temptation because your desire and urge for physical intimacy would increase as your emotional and spiritual intimacy deepened. You would be playing with fire, particularly at a time when you are not yet fully prepared to handle such a serious challenge.
- We could try to fit God's ideas about true love and relationships into the world's pattern (i.e. try to date with a godly mindset), but if God is truly Lord of our lives, He doesn't ask to merely tinker with our approach to romance – He wants to transform it. He has a different and better plan. Why play in the sandbox, when He promises one day to give us the whole beach?!

Note to parents: At this point, we recommend that you discuss with your child what your family philosophy of dating will be in very practical ways. Work together to create specific, realistic guidelines, anticipating as many scenarios as you and your teen can think of. **See the Introduction to this study (pp. 71-73) for suggestions on the types of questions to ask and issues to consider during this discussion.**

With these things in mind, how should I approach guy-girl friendships?

❖ Understand the difference between <u>friendship</u> and <u>intimacy</u>.
  - Friendship is about something (a common goal or interest) other than just the two people in the relationship, while intimacy is about each other.
  - Friends walk side-by-side; lovers stand face-to-face.
  - In your teen years, your intimate relationships should be with your family. God designed the family to meet a young person's emotional needs and to prepare them for the intimacy of marriage.

❖ Be <u>inclusive</u>, not <u>exclusive</u>.
  - Make it a goal to involve as many people as possible in your social activities. If you consistently balk at including other people in activities involving the opposite sex, your true motive likely is not friendship, but something else (like intimacy).
  - If exclusive dating is common in your school or youth group, brainstorm how you and your family can create alternatives.

❖ Seek opportunities to <u>serve</u>, rather than to be <u>entertained</u>.
  - So much of what we do with our leisure time in America is merely consumption and entertainment. Think about the activities that teens typically do with a date – going to dinner, seeing a movie, attending a sporting event – all of which are self-oriented.
  - There is nothing wrong with these activities in and of themselves; they are enjoyable pursuits which can be positive experiences. But a steady diet of these things (i.e. every Saturday night throughout one's teen years) is self-indulgent.
  - Thinking outside the "dating box" creates opportunities for group activities which involve reaching out to a wider social crowd or accomplishing some greater good.
  - Service also gives us opportunities to know friends in a different way and reveals more of their character to us.

❖ Guard your heart.
- Guy-girl friendships don't happen by accident. Men and women are designed to attract each other like magnets. It will take purpose and guardedness to make friendships work, to keep your mind pure, and to keep yourself from premature involvement with people of the opposite sex.
- Prepare ahead of time for the heart to challenge the mind. Pray regularly for God to keep your heart in check, especially when you feel yourself attracted to someone in particular. Have a plan in mind for what you will do if/when you find yourself desiring to move a friendship toward romance before commitment is realistic: For example, talk over your struggle with your parents and/or accountability partner and commit to reducing the amount of time you spend with that person. If the issue has become a stumbling block with the other person involved, consider talking to him or her about your commitment to keeping all your relationships platonic at this stage of your life and your reasons for that. As a last resort, you may need to avoid seeing that person.
- Think through all the consequences of your actions toward anyone of the opposite sex. **Be careful never to lead anyone on** with words or actions that might cause him or her to believe that you would like to pursue a romantic relationship before you are truly ready to pursue one!

What can I do now to prepare for future relationships?

❖ Work on developing Christ-like character qualities.
- Marriage won't transform us into new people. It will act as a mirror, showing us what we already are. Concentrate not just on *finding* the right person one day, but on *becoming* the right person for the person you will eventually marry.

❖ Practice intimacy in other committed relationships, beginning with family.
- We learn to create and maintain intimacy through communication, forgiveness, physical touch (yes, your teen should be hugging his pesky little brother ☺), openness and vulnerability, and spiritual accountability and encouragement with family members.
- God created the family to be an on-going workshop on relationships. Take advantage of the opportunities various members of your family offer for honing people-skills and fostering unconditional love. Good relationships begin at home!

❖ Practice seeking God with others (through prayer, study, and accountability).
- The pursuit of a relationship with God as a couple is foundational for every Christian marriage. Boys, in particular, need to learn how to lead in this area by beginning to facilitate the spiritual growth of others (perhaps a younger sibling, a new Christian, or a children's Sunday school class).
- If your child is hesitant to pray aloud, gently encourage her to practice this within the family and then beyond. The desire, ability, and self-discipline to pray aloud with one's spouse is also foundational to a godly marriage.
- Seek opportunities both in large-group settings (like youth group, family devotions, or a small-group Bible study) and one-on-one (with a parent, sibling, friend, or mentor).

❖ Practice financial responsibility; train to earn a living to provide for your family and care for a home; and develop practical life skills in all areas, including parenting.

- The introduction to this study (p.73) suggests resources you can use to train your teen in these areas; however, you and your spouse (with input from your teen) should put together your own list of skills in which you wish your children to be trained before they leave home. Decide how, when, and with the assistance of whom these goals will be accomplished.

❖ Observe character qualities in others that you would like in a spouse. Develop maturity and life experience that will, among other things, equip you to make a wise choice of a life partner.
- Make a list of people your teen admires. Talk about what it is about these people that attracts your teen and has won her respect.
- Talk about those qualities your teen knows from experience with other people in his life that he would *not* desire in a partner.
- Go back to the follow-up study for Session 2 and review the list of qualities your teen desires most in a spouse; identify those things that are non-negotiables. Such a list will give you a valuable window into the heart of your teen – what is most important to her and what appeals to her about the opposite sex. This list (created before the heart is attached to one specific person) will also be invaluable in the future as an objective standard by which to evaluate potential marriage partners. Encourage your teen to keep this list accessible and to change or add to it as she matures over the next several years.
- Consider keeping a journal about these desired character qualities in a future spouse. Being able to look back at the progression of your thinking over time may help clarify your thoughts and be a valuable tool when you think you may have found "the one."

❖ Serve God and the body of Christ with the unique flexibility, freedom, and focus available to you at this time in your life (without the added responsibilities and distractions of a spouse and children). (See 1 Corinthians 7:32-35.)
- Where/how does your teen enjoy serving others? What kind of example are you as parents setting for your children in this area? Do you regularly seek opportunities for your family to serve together at church, in your community, for a para-church ministry, etc.?
- Brainstorm ways your teen and/or your family could be the hands and feet of Christ to others, in obedience to Matthew 25:35-36. How will you make this a priority?

Conclusion: **God does not want us to develop intimate relationships with non-Christians. And "dating" in today's culture, particularly in the teen years, is often not helpful in preparing you for a committed, lasting relationship with a "suitable" spouse (even if your date is a Christian). Instead, during your teen years pursue "NOBLE" friendships, develop your own character, and begin to identify in others those character qualities that will one day make someone "suitable" as your future spouse.**

Part 5B - Student Discussion Notes

I. Equally Yoked: God's Design for Intimate Relationships

Read 2 Corinthians 6:14-15 and Deuteronomy 22:10. What does it mean to be "yoked" together?

- Being "yoked" together means to be ____________ in a relatively permanent or serious way for the purpose of accomplishing some goal or objective.

What does this passage suggest our attitude and approach intimate relationships (like dating and marriage) with the opposite sex should be?

- It suggests that we should not ___________ (or potentially even date) someone who is not a believer.

Why would God want us to have close and intimate relationships (like close friendship and marriage) only with believers? Think about the implications of the passages above and read 1 Corinthians 15:33 and Psalm 1.

- We cannot associate regularly and closely with others without "__________ ______" on one another.

- The more time we spend and the more intimacy we create with an unbeliever, the stronger the ______________ will be to join him in sin.

- Because Christ must be the center of any vibrant and fulfilling Christian marriage, marrying an unbeliever will necessarily limit the __________ and _______________ of your marriage and limit your _____________ as a couple and a family.

- A spiritual bond with a non-Christian ____________ our bond with Christ.

Read Matthew 5: 13-16. How does God want us to relate to unbelievers?

- We are to be "_______ and ___________" in order to redeem for Christ those in our circle of influence.

II. Friendship and Dating

A. Friendship

If God does not want us to be unequally yoked with unbelievers, what does that mean for the kinds of close friends we should make?

❖ We should choose to have *close* friendships primarily, if not exclusively, with other like-minded ________________.

What are the characteristics of a godly friend?

N________ draw the other into sin. (1 Peter 1:14-16)

O__________ the world's ways. (Romans 12:2; Ephesians 4:22-24)

B_________ each other up. (Ephesians 4:29)

L_______ for what is best in the other, their family, and all things. (Philippians 4:8)

E___________ each other to do the right, loving, and selfless thing. (Hebrews 10:24)

Where would you begin to look for godly friends? Why?

B. Dating

Define "dating." What are its purposes and/or goals?

What do you think might be some benefits of dating?

What do you think may be some drawbacks to dating?

Dating Dangers

1. Dating creates an ________________ environment for evaluating ________________.

2. Dating tends to skip the ____________________ stage of relationships.

3. Dating often mistakes a __________________ relationship for ______________.

4. Dating often leads to ____________________, but not necessarily to ______________.

5. Dating often ________________ a couple from other vital _________________.

6. Dating, in many cases, ______________ young adults from their primary responsibility of preparing for the future.

7. Dating can cause ____________________ with God's gift of __________________.

III. Application to Me

What will my approach to dating be?

With these things in mind, how should I approach guy-girl friendships?

- ❖ Understand the difference between ___________ and ____________.
- ❖ Be ___________, not ______________.
- ❖ Seek opportunities to _________, rather than to be ______________.
- ❖ ___________ your ___________.

What can I do now to prepare for future relationships?

- ❖ Work on developing Christ-like _____________ qualities.
- ❖ Practice ________________ in other committed relationships, beginning with _____________.
- ❖ Practice seeking God with others (through _________, __________, and _______________).
- ❖ Practice _______________ responsibility; _____________ to earn a living to provide for your family and care for a home; and develop practical ________ __________ in all areas, including parenting.
- ❖ Observe _____________ ______________ in others that you would like in a spouse. Develop ____________ and _________ ___________ that will, among other things, equip you to make a wise choice of a life partner.
- ❖ Serve God and the body of Christ with the unique _________________, _______________, and ______________ available to you at this time in your life (without the added responsibilities and distractions of a spouse and children). (See 1 Cor. 7:32-35.)

Conclusion: **God does not want us to develop intimate relationships with non-Christians. And "dating" in today's culture, particularly in the teen years, is often not helpful in preparing you for a committed, lasting relationship with a "suitable" spouse (even if your date is a Christian). Instead, during your teen years pursue "NOBLE" friendships, develop your own character, and begin to identify in others those character qualities that will one day make someone "suitable" as your future spouse.**

Part 5C - Student Follow-up Study

***Scripture Memory**: 2 Corinthians 6:14-15, Song of Songs 3:7b, Ecclesiastes 3:1,7b*

1. The stories of Ruth & Boaz and Isaac & Rebekah are interesting examples of alternatives to "dating" as a method of seeking a husband or wife. Read each story again, and answer the corresponding questions.

   <u>Ruth and Boaz</u> (Ruth 2 – 4)

   What was it that initially attracted Boaz to Ruth? (2:10-12)

   What was the goal of Ruth and Naomi in pursuing Boaz as a potential husband? (3:1)

   What was it about Ruth that ultimately attracted Boaz to her (made her "suitable")? (3:10-11)

   What kind of character did each have? (2:11-12; 3:10-11,18)

   What lessons can you learn from this story about dating and looking for your future spouse?

Isaac and Rebekah (Genesis 24)

Where did Abraham want his servant to go to find a wife for his son Isaac? Why? (24:3-4)

What was the test that the servant used to determine who would be "suitable" as a wife for Isaac? (24:12-14)

What does this reveal the servant was looking for in Isaac's future wife? How much did "looks" (outward beauty) matter?

What kind of character did Rebekah demonstrate by her actions with Abraham's servant? (24:17-28)

What was the result of the servant's efforts? (24:66-67)

What lessons can you learn from this story about dating and looking for your future spouse?

2. There are also examples in the Bible of approaches to dating and finding a "suitable" spouse that did not work well. Read each story, and answer the corresponding questions.

Samson and the Philistine Woman (Judges 14)

Where did Samson go to look for a wife, and what criteria did he use for making his decision? (14:1-4)

What, apparently, was it that attracted him to the Philistine woman? (14:1,7)

What kind of character did each have? (14:15-17)

What was the result of this dating/courtship? (14:18-20) Why did it fail?

What lessons can you learn from this story about dating and looking for your future spouse?

Shechem and Dinah (Genesis 34)

What did Dinah do initially? (34:1) Was this wise? Based on the whole story, why or why not?

What was the basis of Shechem's interest in Dinah? (34:2)

What was the primary basis of the relationship and his desire to marry her? (34:3-4)

What did his sexual obsession with her cause him to do? (34:2, 11-12)

What were the long-term results of Shechem's sin? (34:13-19, 24-29)

What lessons can you learn from this story about dating and looking for your future spouse?

3. As a result of this study, are there any decisions or new commitments you have made or want to make about dating and your approach to finding a "suitable" spouse?

4. Write out how you would explain your philosophy of dating to a friend or interested adult. Take your time, think through it carefully, and write it out fully. (Use a separate sheet of paper if necessary)

5. Are there any questions or concerns you have following this study that you want to discuss further with us?

Part 5D - Parent Follow-up Guide

***Scripture Memory**: 2 Corinthians 6:14-15, Song of Songs 3:7b, Ecclesiastes 3:1,7b*

1. **The stories of Ruth & Boaz and Isaac & Rebekah are interesting examples of alternatives to "dating" as a method of seeking a husband or wife. Read each story again, and answer the corresponding questions.**

<u>Ruth and Boaz</u> (Ruth 2 – 4)

What was it that initially attracted Boaz to Ruth? (2:10-12)

- Her faithfulness to her mother-in-law when she followed her mother-in-law from a foreign land after their husbands died
- Her choice to trust the God of Israel rather than her own foreign gods

What was the goal of Ruth and Naomi in pursuing Boaz as a potential husband? (3:1)

- To find a home where she would be well provided for

What was it about Ruth that ultimately attracted Boaz to her (made her "suitable")? (3:10-11)

- She did not run after the younger men, whether rich or poor (did not pursue fun or excitement and did not value youth over character).
- She was a woman of noble character.

What kind of character did each have? (2:11-12; 3:10-11,18)

- Ruth had a "noble" character; she sought after the true God and provided for her family in time of need.
- Boaz was a man of his word – a man of integrity – who pursued something until it was completed.

What lessons can you learn from this story about dating and looking for your future spouse?

Answers will vary but may include:

- Don't pursue appearances, money, or other superficial things.
- Instead, look for someone who has a "noble character" and is "suitable" for me.
- Look for someone who is a Christian.
- Look for someone with whom I can build a home that will adequately provide for everyone.

<u>Isaac and Rebekah</u> (Genesis 24)

Where did Abraham want his servant to go to find a wife for his son Isaac? Why? (24:3-4)

- Abraham did not want his servant to choose a wife for Isaac from the Canaanites, but from among his own country and relatives.
- Abraham did not want Isaac to be "yoked" with someone from the local culture because he knew Isaac might then be tempted to follow the gods of the Canaanites and assimilate the local culture. He knew that bringing back a wife from his original home country would help to insulate her and Isaac from the influences of any pagan religious practices.

What was the test that the servant used to determine who would be "suitable" as a wife for Isaac? (24:12-14)

- He did not choose a test based on beauty or apparent wealth. Instead, he tested whether she would draw water at his request and then go the extra mile to offer to draw water for his camels.
- He used a test of character.

What does this reveal the servant was looking for in Isaac's future wife? How much did "looks" (outward beauty) matter?

- It was a test that would reveal true inner character, because drawing water for all of his camels would involve a great sacrifice of time and a great deal of work.
- Looks, which appeared not to matter at all, were not as important as character and inner beauty, .

What kind of character did Rebekah demonstrate by her actions with Abraham's servant? (24:17-28)

- Rebekah demonstrated courtesy, selflessness, kindness, and hospitality.
- She did not hesitate but "quickly lowered her jar."
- She said she would draw water for his camels "until they [had] finished drinking" – which probably would have been a significant amount of water because of the long journey they had just completed.
- She did not hesitate to offer food and shelter for the evening (hospitality) even though this would again involve work on her part.
- She went immediately to tell her parents about what had happened, indicating that she had a good relationship with her parents.

What was the result of the servant's efforts? (24:66-67)

- Rebekah and Isaac were married. Isaac loved her (true love vs. infatuation), and she comforted him after his mother's death.

What lessons can you learn from this story about dating and looking for your future spouse?

Answers will vary but may include:

- Pursue someone who shares my faith.

  (*Note to parents:* This might be a good time to discuss with your teen what tenets of his theology he considers non-negotiable.)

- Pursue inner beauty (noble character), not outward appearance or wealth, in my future spouse.
- Consider pursuing someone from my parents' circle of close friends/community/ sphere of influence because their values are likely to be similar to mine.

2. **There are also examples in the Bible of approaches to dating and finding a "suitable" spouse that did not work well.**

   Read each story, and answer the corresponding questions.

Samson and the Philistine Woman (Judges 14)

Where did Samson go to look for a wife, and what criteria did he use for making his decision? (14:1-4)

- He went among the pagan Philistines, rather than his own people, the Israelites.
- Apparently, he based his decisions on what he had "seen" (outward appearance – he "saw a young Philistine woman").

What, apparently, was it that attracted him to the Philistine woman? (14:1,7)

- Her looks/appearance
- Whatever he could have learned by simply talking with her (apparently once)
- Infatuation/lust, not true love

What kind of character did each have? (14:15-17)

- She was deceptive and manipulative. Her allegiances were more to her own family/people than to her future husband.
- He was less than honorable with her family. The riddle he proposed was simply a way to get more money and possessions for himself.

What was the result of this dating/courtship? (14:18-20) Why did it fail?

- There was no time for a friendship to be established and their love to mature and be tested.
- Samson became embroiled in a dispute with the woman's family, the two never married, and the Philistine woman was given in marriage to someone else.
- It probably failed because it was based on outward appearances (infatuation or lust), rather than on a true love based on a knowledge of and appreciation for the character (inner beauty) of the other.

What lessons can you learn from this story about dating and looking for your future spouse?

- Look for a Christian spouse; don't date or court a non-Christian.
- Begin looking for my spouse among people in my and my parents' circle of Christian friends.
- Spend a lot of time getting to know the person's character before making any decisions about the future.
- Focus on the heart, not outward appearances.

Shechem and Dinah (Genesis 34)

What did Dinah do initially? (34:1) Was this wise? Based on the whole story, why or why not?

- She went walking around alone, visiting girls from other towns.
- This was not wise because it left her vulnerable to strangers.

What was the basis of Shechem's interest in Dinah? (34:2)

- It was a purely physical attraction (lust/infatuation).

What was the primary basis of the relationship and his desire to marry her? (34:3-4)

- While verse 3 says he "loved" her, his later actions proved that he had mistaken lust/infatuation and physical attraction for "true love."

What did his sexual obsession with her cause him to do? (34:2, 11-12)

- He raped her.
- He was willing to do anything to possess her; he lost all reason and balance in his decision-making.

What were the long-term results of Shechem's sin? (34:13-19, 24-29)

- Shechem's sin placed him and his kin in an extremely compromising situation and ultimately led to the death of not only Shechem, but every male in his community. All their possessions, women, and children were taken away by Dinah's brothers as plunder.
- Dinah was disgraced and had no future.

What lessons can you learn from this story about dating and looking for your future spouse?

- Avoid guys/girls who are simply "shopping around" for fun and excitement or for male/female companionship.
- Base my decisions on true love, not lust/infatuation. Think long-term.
- Don't make hasty decisions about getting married, and don't be willing to give up everything (including my principles and character) to marry someone.

3. **As a result of this study, are there any decisions or new commitments you have made or want to make about dating and your approach to finding a "suitable" spouse?**

4. **Write out how you would explain your philosophy of dating to a friend or interested adult. Take your time, think through it carefully, and write it out fully. (Use a separate sheet of paper if necessary.)**

5. **Are there any questions or concerns you have following this study that you want to discuss further with us?**

Session 6:
The Covenant of Sexual Purity

Session Purpose and Themes

Session Summary:

The purity covenant which you may choose to invite your teen to make at the end of this session is the consummation of the previous five sessions. In preparation for making this covenant, we examine what a covenant is, why it is serious and important, and how covenants are modeled in the Bible. Then we explore each element of the purity covenant included in this workbook so that your teen will know exactly what he is committing to, should he decide to sign it. (If you decide to write your own covenant, you will need to change the final portion of the outline to explain each element of the covenant *you* have created.) Finally, we introduce the concept of the purity ring as a visual symbol of the commitment made in the written covenant.

Session Themes:

- "Covenants" are solemn, spoken or written commitments between two people which are typically sealed with a symbolic act or token. There are numerous examples of "covenants" in the Bible, both among men and between God and man.
- A covenant of sexual purity is a covenant between you and God in which you commit to be faithful to God's standards of sexual purity (for both body and mind) and trust God's promises to empower you, through His grace and the Holy Spirit, to keep that commitment.
- A covenant of sexual purity should not be entered into lightly, but only after considerable prayer and a clear, heartfelt conviction that God's standard for sexual purity is your true desire.
- A covenant of sexual purity, when coupled with a purity ring, anticipates the marriage covenant you will someday make with the "suitable" spouse God has in store for you.

Hints for a More Effective Study

- Emphasize with your teen that covenants are serious undertakings that should be entered into only after extended prayer and examination of the heart. In signing the covenant, your teen will be committing to live purposefully by the standards God has established for sexual purity. We suggest telling her that you don't expect her to make a decision today or even next week. In fact, because of the seriousness of this commitment, you will ask her to pray, review the past five lessons, and take whatever time she finds necessary to make this important choice. She can then let you know when she has reached a decision.
- Consider requiring your teen, once he has made a decision, to provide you with a written list of reasons for and implications (costs and benefits) of his decision. If the decision is to make a covenant, this list will give you confidence that he has given the decision sufficient thought and fully understands the seriousness of the commitment he is making. If the decision is not to make a covenant at this time, it will give you a starting point for a continuing dialogue with him about these important issues.
- We have provided you with sample certificates (based on the principles we have explored in the past five sessions) which could be signed, as is, by your son (page 103) or daughter (page 104) and you as parents. (We had our son's younger brother sign the certificate, as well, in acknowledgement of his desire to support his brother in fulfilling his covenant.) You could then frame the certificate to hang on her

bedroom wall as a daily reminder of her commitment. You may also want to consider tailoring the model we have provided to your child's unique situation, or even allowing her to write her own covenant, with your input and approval.

- If your teen desires to make a covenant of sexual purity, we encourage you to celebrate in a memorable way! When you make a big deal out of your child's covenant, you confirm the importance of the decision he has made. In our home, we served a special dinner of all of our son's favorite foods on our best china. After dinner, our son read the covenant aloud and we all signed it. We then presented him with his purity ring (which he had helped design but had not yet seen in its finished form). We believe that this is one of the most important commitments (after a decision to acknowledge Christ as Savior) that our children will make, so we wanted the signing of the covenant to be a memorable event. We wanted our son to see in a concrete way how important his decision was to us, which we conveyed in part by the time and resources (including money) we spent preparing for it. We believe it is important to include siblings in the celebration so that they can learn from the example of their brother or sister and begin to think about and look forward to their own commitment to purity.

Precautions

- If, after a couple of weeks, you have not heard from your teen, gently follow up with her to make sure she is still focusing on the decision she needs to make.
- Be sure to emphasize with your teen that his covenant of sexual purity is not broken or annulled by a single stumble (Psalm 37:23-24). There are always consequences for sin, and if your child breaks his covenant he will likely be disciplined by his Heavenly Father (perhaps through natural consequences, perhaps through you). But God will freely and graciously forgive the sin of a truly repentant person and empower him or her again to live a life of faithful obedience to His standards. (Think about how many times Israel broke their covenant with God and how many times God forgave them and gave them the opportunity to keep their part of the covenant once again!) It is only a persistent or deliberate decision to live a lifestyle contrary to God's standards that will break or annul that covenant.

Additional Resources

Durfield, Richard C. *Raising Them Chaste: A Practical Strategy for Helping Your Teen Wait Till Marriage.* Minneapolis: Bethany House Publishers, 1991.

Wilson, Douglas. *Her Hand in Marriage: Biblical Courtship in the Modern World.* Moscow, Idaho: Canon Press, 1997.

Part 6A - Parent Discussion Guide

Introductory comments:

- Because you have worked hard and successfully completed the study on sexual purity, you are being given the opportunity to make a COVENANT (or commitment) of sexual purity before God.
- Because covenants are a very serious and solemn commitment that should not be taken lightly, we want to spend some time exploring with you the nature of this kind of commitment.
- First, we will examine what the Bible has to say about covenants generally, and then we will discuss what a "covenant of sexual purity" means and involves on your part.

I. WHAT IS A "COVENANT"?

A. Definition

❖ A solemn and spoken <u>commitment</u> and <u>promise</u> between two people that is typically sealed with a symbolic act and/or token

❖ In its simplest form, a contract, <u>agreement</u>, or treaty between two parties

B. Examples in the Bible

1. Among Men

❖ Laban and Jacob (Genesis 31:36-55)
- When Jacob left Laban at God's command after marrying Leah and Rachel, Laban pursued him in anger because someone (Rachel) had taken his household gods.
- Laban and Jacob made a covenant between the two of them (v. 44) that neither would cross into the other's area to harm the other (vv. 52-53).
- Each person promised (and Jacob took an oath) to adhere to this covenant, which they sealed with an act (eating a meal together) (v. 54) and a symbol (a heap of stones) (vv. 45-46). Jacob also offered a sacrifice as a seal of the covenant (v. 54).

❖ King Asa and Ben Hadad (1 Kings 15:16-20)
- Asa, king of Judah (the Southern kingdom) was at war with Baasha, king of Israel (the Northern kingdom) because Baasha had fortified Ramah and sealed off entry into Judah (vv. 16-17).
- King Asa called on Ben-Hadad, king of Aram (Damascus) and entered into a treaty with him not to fight (and also calling on him to break his treaty with Baasha) (vv. 19-20).
- King Asa sealed the treaty with a gift of gold and silver (v. 19).

2. Between God and Man

- These covenants are different than those between men because:
  - The other party is the God of the universe, not a mere man.

  - God graciously commits Himself to bless and care for His children. (Nahum 1:7; 1Peter 5:7)
    Nahum 1:7 – "The Lord is good, a refuge in times of trouble. He cares for those who trust in Him."
    1 Peter 5:7 – "Cast all your anxiety on Him, because He cares for you."

  - He enables us, trusting in His grace, to respond with a commitment of our own that He will empower us to keep. (Philippians 1:6)
    Philippians 1:6 – "being confident of this, that He who began a good work in you will carry it on to completion until the day of Christ Jesus."

  - Unlike men, God is completely faithful to keep His promises. (2 Timothy 2:13; Heb. 10:23)
    2 Timothy 2:13 – "If we are faithless, He will remain faithful, for He cannot disown Himself."
    Hebrews 10:23 – "Let us hold unswervingly to the hope we profess, for He who promised is faithful."

- Examples:
  God and Noah (Genesis 9:8-17)
  - Following the flood, God promised (covenanted with) Noah that He would never again destroy the earth by a flood (v. 11).
  - God sealed that covenant with the symbol of a rainbow (vv. 12-17).
  - God has never broken that covenant.

  God and Abraham/Israel (Genesis 15:1-21; 17:1-14)
  - God covenanted with Abraham that He would make him into a great nation, as numerous as the stars in the sky and the sand on the beach (15:5), and that He would give his descendents the land of Canaan (15:7).
  - God sealed this covenant with the symbol of a firepot moving through the sacrifices of a heifer, goat, and ram (15:10, 17-18) and then with the symbol of circumcision (17:9-14).
  - God kept that covenant by making a great nation of Israel, preserving the Jewish nation for over 2000 years, and establishing the Church today.

3. Christ's Ultimate Covenant with Us

- God made a new covenant of salvation with us through the death and resurrection of Jesus. (Matthew 26:28)

  Matthew 26:28 – "This is my blood of the covenant, which is poured out for many for the forgiveness of sins."

  - In this covenant, God has made a loving commitment to forgive our sin and enable us to walk in fellowship with Him.

- ❖ He has sealed that covenant with the symbols of baptism and communion. (Romans 6:3-4; 1 Corinthians 11:26)

  Romans 6:3-4 – "Or don't you know that all of us who were baptized into Christ Jesus were baptized into His death? We were therefore buried with Him through baptism into death in order that, just as Christ was raised from the dead through the glory of the Father, we too may live a new life."

  1 Corinthians 11:26 – "For whenever you eat this bread and drink this cup, you proclaim the Lord's death until He comes."

- ❖ He further sealed that covenant by the indwelling of the Holy Spirit, whose power makes it possible to fulfill our commitment to live holy and pleasing lives. (Ephesians 1:13b-14; Acts 1:8)

  Ephesians 1:13b-14 – "Having believed, you were marked in Him with a seal, the promised Holy Spirit, who is a deposit guaranteeing our inheritance until the redemption of those who are God's possession – to the praise of His glory."

  Acts 1:8 – " 'But you will receive power when the Holy Spirit comes on you; and you will be my witnesses in Jerusalem, and in all Judea and Samaria, and to the ends of the earth.' "

II. THE COVENANT OF SEXUAL PURITY

- ❖ A solemn and very serious public commitment to love God, honor Him, and obey His will in all things, particularly sexual purity

- ❖ A prelude to your marriage commitment to your future spouse
  - ➢ In marriage, you covenant to "forsake all others" for your spouse.
  - ➢ In the purity covenant, you commit to remain sexually pure (forsake all others) for the spouse God has in store for you.

- ❖ In gratitude for God's good gift of sexual love, you covenant with (promise) God to:
  - ➢ Remain faithful and obedient to God in all things
  - ➢ Dedicate your sexuality to God's glory and control, both while single (abstinence) and while married (faithfulness)
  - ➢ Keep that gift pure (body, mind, and emotions), forsaking all others for the spouse God has chosen specifically for you
  - ➢ Pursue "NOBLE" friendships, focusing on developing your own Christian character and leaving dating or courting relationships for an appropriate season in your life
  - ➢ Be motivated by true love, not lust or infatuation, when considering a relationship with someone of the opposite sex
  - ➢ Pursue a "suitable" Christian spouse at the appropriate time, someone who possesses the carefully considered character qualities you desire in a spouse
  - ➢ Be accountable to and seek the wisdom of your parents and other adult mentors about your promises

- ❖ A "covenant" is not permanently or irrevocably broken by one or more failures.
  - ➢ God commits to forgive and restore us when we sin and repent and seek forgiveness. (1 John 1:9)
  - ➢ A covenant is "annulled" (or broken) by a persistent desire to live a lifestyle contrary to God's promises.
  - ➢ The consequences, however, of breaking a covenant – even temporarily – are real. God promises to discipline us in order to bring us into fuller obedience to Him. (See Hebrews 12:5, 10-11.)

III. YOUR COVENANT OF PURITY

A. The Symbol of the Purity Ring

- The ring is an ancient symbol of the marriage vow, of faithfulness to one person for life.
- If you decide to make a covenant of purity with God, we would like to present you with a purity ring as a visual reminder of and seal on your commitment to pursue sexual purity.
- Purity is not a point on a line to which we try to come as close as we can without going past it. It is a *direction* which we want to pursue with a passion! A purity ring will remind you daily of the commitment you have made and the direction in which you want to walk.
- The purity ring will also serve as a foreshadowing of your marriage covenant. By this ring, you make a covenant to forsake any sexual intimacy until you become one with your spouse on your wedding night.
- Finally, the purity ring will be a reminder that your future is in God's hands, and if He has marriage in mind for you, He will provide the right partner at the right time.
- At your wedding (or on your wedding night), you may decide to give your purity ring to your spouse as a symbol of your commitment of purity to him or her years earlier, in exchange for a new wedding ring which will symbolize your marriage covenant with him or her and with God.

B. Your Covenant of Sexual Purity

- Now you need to take some time to think and pray over this covenant. As we have just discussed, entering into a covenant like this is not to be taken lightly. If/when you believe you are ready to sign the covenant, fully understanding the seriousness and importance of what you are doing, come to us and let us know that you would like to move forward. At that point, we will set aside a date and time to sign the covenant and to present you with your purity ring. If you do not believe you are ready to sign the covanent, or want to change it, we want to talk with you about that too.
- Whatever you decide, we want you to come with a written list of reasons for your decision, as well as what you believe will be the implications (potential costs and benefits) of your decision.

Part 6B - Student Discussion Notes

I. WHAT IS A "COVENANT"?

A. Definition

- ❖ A solemn and spoken ____________ and ____________ between two people that is typically sealed with a symbolic act and/or token
- ❖ In its simplest form, a contract, _______________, or treaty between two parties

B. Examples in the Bible

1. Among Men
   - ❖ Laban and Jacob (Genesis 31:36-55)
   - ❖ King Asa and Ben Hadad (1 Kings 15:16-20)

2. Between God and Man
   - ❖ These covenants are different than those between men because:
     - ➢ The other party is the _________ of the universe, not a mere man.
     - ➢ God graciously commits himself to ________ and ______ for His children. (Nahum 1:7; 1 Peter 5:7)
     - ➢ He enables us, trusting in His grace, to ____________ with a commitment of our own that He will empower us to keep. (Philippians 1:6)
     - ➢ Unlike men, God is completely ____________ to keep His promises. (2 Timothy 2:13; Hebrews 10:23)
   - ❖ Examples:
God and Noah (Genesis 9:8-17)
God and Abraham/Israel (Genesis 15:1-21; 17:1-14)

3. Christ's Ultimate Covenant with Us
   - ❖ God made a new covenant of _______________ with us through the death and resurrection of Jesus. (Matthew 26:28)
     - ➢ In this covenant, God has made a loving commitment to ___________ our sin and _____________ us to walk in fellowship with Him.
   - ❖ He has sealed that covenant with the symbols of __________ and ____________. (Romans 6:3-4; 1 Corinthians 11:26)
   - ❖ He further sealed that covenant by the indwelling of the _________ ____________, whose ____________ makes it possible to fulfill our commitment to live holy and pleasing lives. (Ephesians 1:13b-14; Acts 1:8)

II. THE COVENANT OF SEXUAL PURITY

- A solemn and very serious public commitment to _______ God, ____________ Him, and __________ His will in all things, particularly sexual purity

- A prelude to your ____________ commitment to your future spouse

  - In marriage, you covenant to "forsake all others" for your __________.

  - In the purity covenant, you commit to remain ______________ pure (forsake all others) for the spouse God has in store for you.

- In gratitude for God's good gift of sexual love, you covenant with (promise) God to:

  - Remain ___________ and ____________ to God in all things
  - Dedicate your ______________ to God's glory and control, both while single (abstinence) and while married (faithfulness)
  - Keep that gift __________ (body, mind, and emotions), forsaking all others for the spouse God has chosen specifically for you
  - Pursue "NOBLE" _______________, focusing on developing your own Christian ______________ and leaving dating or courting relationships for an appropriate _____________ in your life
  - Be motivated by _______ _______, not _______ or ____________, when considering a relationship with someone of the opposite sex
  - Pursue a "__________" Christian spouse at the appropriate time, someone who possesses the carefully considered character _______________ you desire in a spouse
  - Be ____________ to and seek the wisdom of your parents and other adult mentors about your promises

- A "covenant" is not permanently or irrevocably ____________ by one or more failures.

  - God commits to __________ and ___________ us when we sin and repent and seek forgiveness. (1 John 1:9)
  - A covenant is "_____________" (or broken) by a persistent desire to live a lifestyle contrary to God's promises.
  - The ______________, however, of breaking a covenant – even temporarily – are real. God promises to ____________ us in order to bring us into fuller obedience to Him. (See Hebrews 12:5, 10-11.)

III. YOUR COVENANT OF PURITY

A. The Symbol of the Purity Ring

B. Your Covenant of Sexual Purity

MY PURITY COVENANT

"Flee from sexual immorality. All other sins a man commits are outside his body, but he who sins sexually sins against his own body. Do you not know that your body is the temple of the Holy Spirit, who is in you, whom you have received from God? You are not your own; you were bought with a price. Therefore honor God with your body."

I Corinthians 6:18-20

In gratitude for God's good gift of sexual love, I covenant with God to:

- **R**emain faithful and obedient to God in all things;
- **D**edicate my sexuality to God's glory and control, both while single (abstinence) and while married (faithfulness);
- **K**eep that gift pure (body, mind, and emotions), forsaking all others for the helpmate God has chosen for me;
- **P**ursue "NOBLE" friendships, focusing on developing my own Christian character and leaving other relationships for an appropriate season in my life, when I am ready for marriage.
- **B**e motivated by true love, not lust or infatuation, when considering a relationship with a woman;
- **P**ursue a "suitable" Christian spouse at the appropriate time, someone who meets the carefully considered character qualities I desire in a mate; and
- **B**e accountable to and seek the wisdom of my parents and other adult mentors about my promises.

The ring is an ancient symbol of the marriage vow, of faithfulness to one particular person for life. The ring that I receive today serves as a foreshadowing of my marriage covenant. On my wedding day, I will give my purity ring to my wife as a symbol of my commitment of purity to her before I even met her and will exchange with her wedding rings, symbolizing our covenant of purity in marriage with each other and God.

Made this ____ *day of* ________ *in the year* ____ *by*

______________________________,

witnessed & supported by ______________________

and ______________________.

MY PURITY COVENANT

"Flee from sexual immorality. All other sins a man commits are outside his body, but he who sins sexually sins against his own body. Do you not know that your body is the temple of the Holy Spirit, who is in you, whom you have received from God? You are not your own; you were bought with a price. Therefore honor God with your body."

I Corinthians 6:18-20

In gratitude for God's good gift of sexual love, I covenant with God to:

- **R**emain faithful and obedient to God in all things;
- **D**edicate my sexuality to God's glory and control, both while single (abstinence) and while married (faithfulness);
- **K**eep that gift pure (body, mind, and emotions), forsaking all others for the helpmate God has chosen for me;
- **P**ursue "NOBLE" friendships, focusing on developing my own Christian character and leaving other relationships for an appropriate season in my life, when I am ready for marriage.
- **B**e motivated by true love, not lust or infatuation, when considering a relationship with a man;
- **P**ursue a "suitable" Christian spouse at the appropriate time, someone who meets the carefully considered character qualities I desire in a mate; and
- **B**e accountable to and seek the wisdom of my parents and other adult mentors about my promises.

The ring is an ancient symbol of the marriage vow, of faithfulness to one particular person for life. The ring that I receive today serves as a foreshadowing of my marriage covenant. On my wedding day, I will give my purity ring to my husband as a symbol of my commitment of purity to him before I even met him and will exchange with him wedding rings, symbolizing our covenant of purity in marriage with each other and God.

Made this ____ *day of* ________ *in the year* ____ *by*

______________________________________,

witnessed & supported by ____________________________

and ______________________________.

Appendix I - Sample Letter to Your Child

Dear Andrew:

We would like to invite you on an adventure with us that will take you to places you have never been before! You've noticed all the physical changes taking place in your body. Along with those, you have also begun to experience changes in how you feel, what is important to you, and what you most look forward to in the future. As your parents, we have been appointed by God to guide you through all these physical, emotional, and spiritual changes. And right now we recognize that it is time to introduce the topics of sexuality, purity, dating, and marriage to you in a direct, specific, and biblical way.

Sometimes these are subjects that kids and parents feel awkward talking about. But we want you to discuss everything that is important to you with us honestly and openly. We want the three of us to become comfortable talking with one another about things like signs of puberty, social situations, and new temptations that may seem frightening, but that with the power of the Spirit within you, our support, and the accountability of godly friends, will become opportunities to defeat Satan and glorify God.

As you reach your high school years, you will at times undoubtedly feel different from other kids. You know from your own experience that different families, even Christian families, have different approaches to things like movies and music and boy-girl relationships. You also know that some people claim to be Christians but truly care more about being like everybody else than about being like Christ. As you grow through your teen years, many of your peers will likely take a different approach to dating and sexual purity; however, we want you to stand out for Christ! And that means being different (being salt and light to our culture) – because the Bible tells us we can't love God and love the world at the same time.

It won't always be easy to do the right thing. At this time of your life, perhaps more than any other, it will sometimes be hard to "stand alone" because it is natural in your teen years to feel insecure and to place great importance on what other people think. But you have the ultimate and intimate security of knowing who you are in Christ. You know you are totally loved by Him just the way you are. And you will never stand alone, because along with Jesus, we, your family, will always stand with you. The blessings you experience will *always, abundantly* outweigh the sacrifices God calls you to make.

God wants you to be honest with *Him* about how you feel too. He doesn't want you to go through the motions of saying what you think He wants to hear. He wants you to tell Him how you really feel and to struggle through it with Him in prayer and study until He has empowered you to do the right thing.

Sometimes it will take a step of faith to do what the Bible or your parents tell you is right. You may not always see at the moment how or why a particular course of action is the best way to go. But always remind yourself that your mom and dad have had life experience that you have not yet had. We love you and *always* have your best interests at heart. And the course that looks right to man (especially a young and inexperienced man) often leads to death. God knows all, and the rules He gives us in His Word are designed to protect and bless us, not to deprive us of any good thing. We plan to meet with you once a week after Ryan is in bed to do a study on each of the following topics:

- Physical Changes and Sexual Love – "Nuts & Bolts"
- God's Design for Sexual Love: Purity When Single and Faithfulness When Married
- Lust and Infatuation vs. True Love
- Integrity, Self-Control, and Sexual Purity
- Who and When Should I Date?
- The Covenant of Sexual Purity

The three of us will work through these together in a series of one- to two-hour sessions. At the end of each study, you will be asked to do a brief follow-up study and short Scripture memory about that session topic. In addition to completing the follow-up study by our next session, your main responsibility is simply to come with a sense of anticipation, an open mind and heart, a willingness to talk openly and ask questions, and a desire to learn God's way in these important and sensitive areas of growing up. Before our first session, we would like you to spend some time praying about this study and writing down specific questions about purity, dating, sex, and marriage. We will do our best to answer your questions over the next few weeks. We are really looking forward to making this journey together and to what God has in store for all three of us!

Love, Mom & Dad

Appendix IIa
Male Reproductive Anatomy

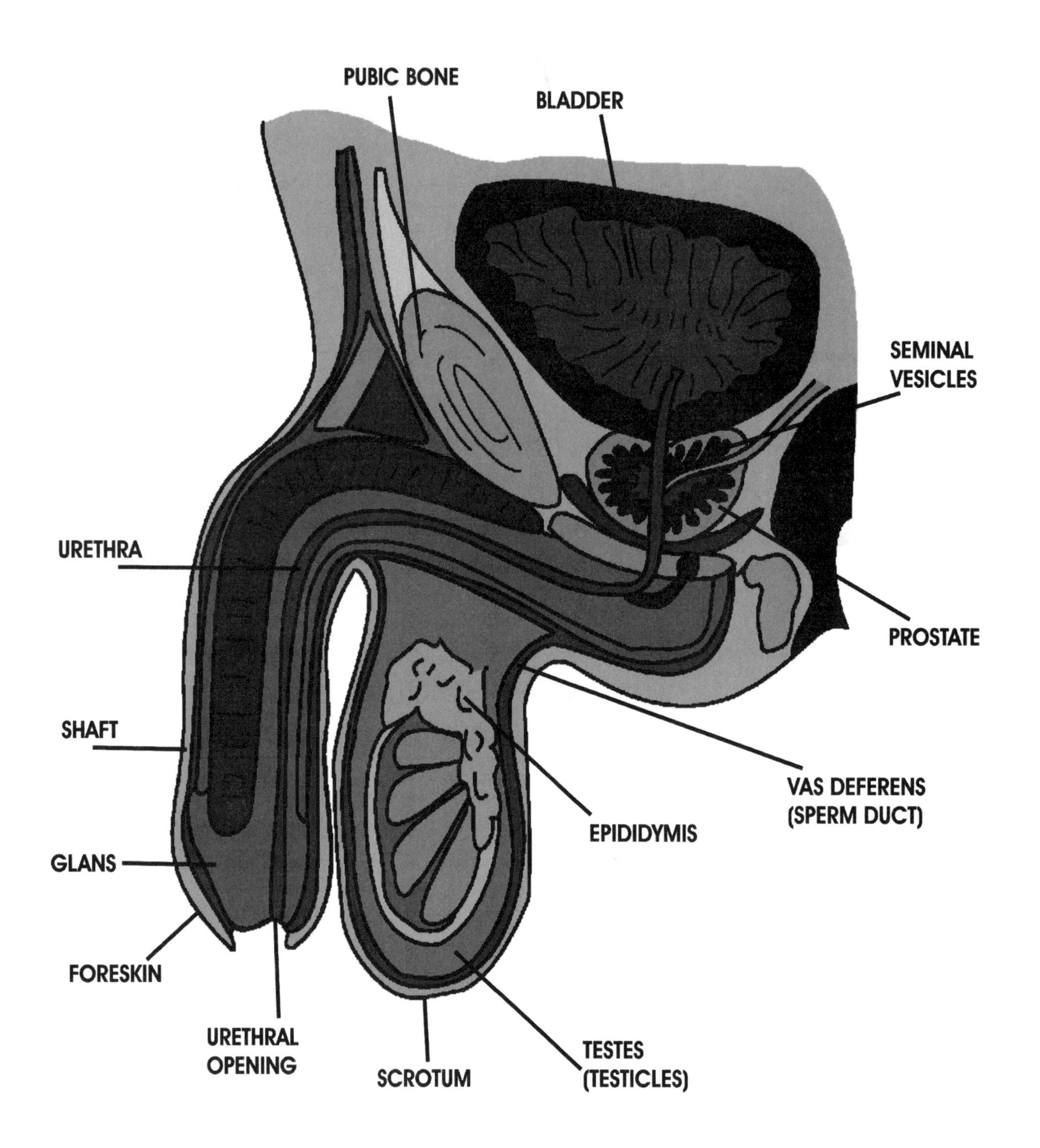

Appendix IIb
Female Reproductive Anatomy

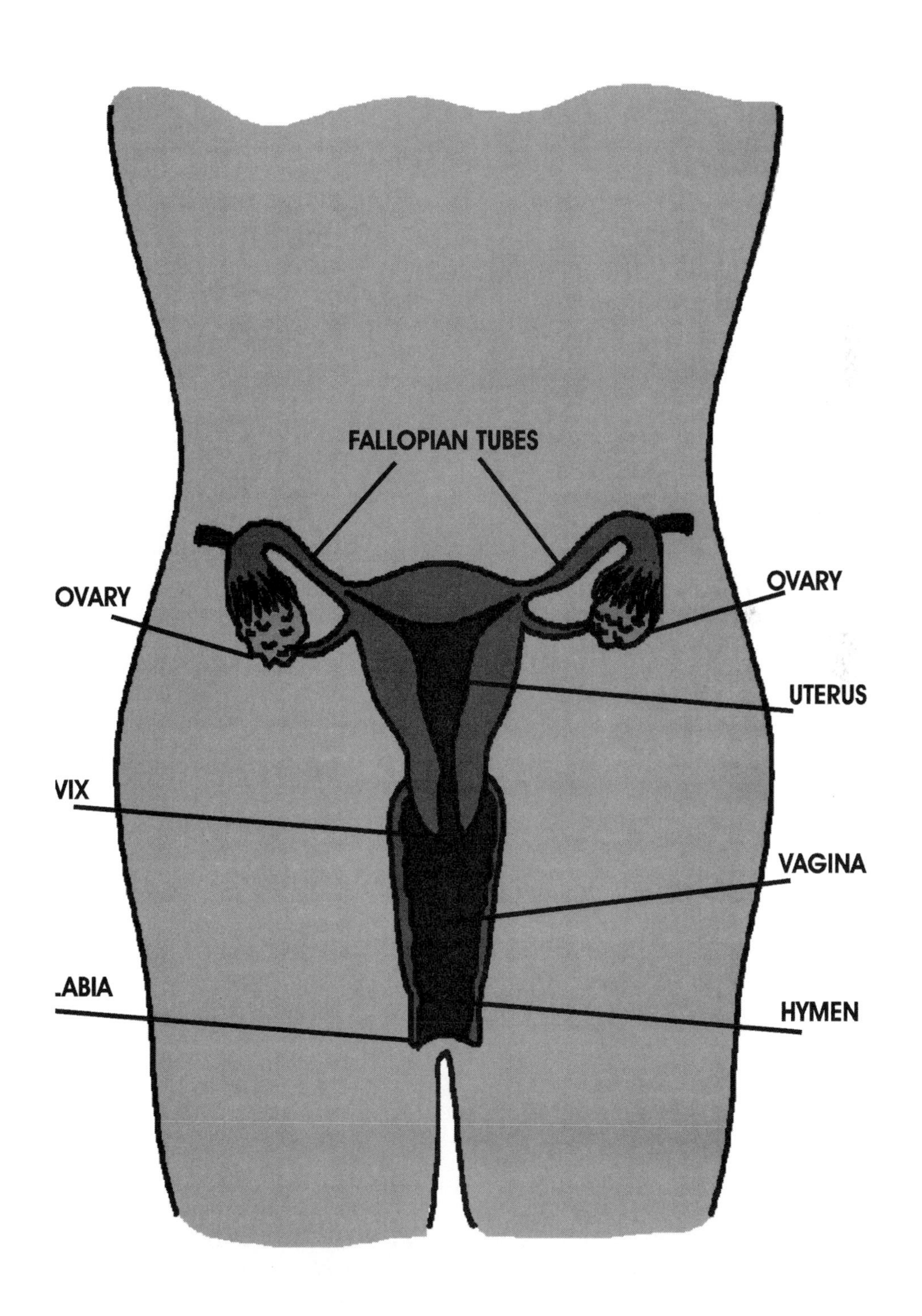

MALACHI GLOBAL FOUNDATION

This book is an integral part of the growing list of resources endorsed and distributed by the Malachi Global Foundation. Our foundation exists to equip parents and other mentors to reach and successfully love and disciple the next generation in fulfillment of Malachi 4:6.

Malachi Global Foundation sponsors many activities including:

- Weekend men's retreats sponsored by local churches
- Fatherhood community seminars
- A 12-week course for parents on lifelong mentoring, intentional blessing and rites of passage
- An international television program on fatherhood
- A resource library for books, tapes, CDs and DVDs
- Outdoor adventure retreats for fathers and sons, fathers and daughters, and blended families.

MALACHI GLOBAL FOUNDATION

CONTACT INFORMATION:

Malachi Global Foundation
1550 Collins Lane
Midland, MI 48640

Tel. 989.698.0468
Fax 989.698.0469
Toll Free 877.MALACHI

info@malachiglobal.org
malachioffice@aol.com
www.malachiglobal.org

Sexual sin is destroying our families, our nation and our children.

Be part of the solution.

Share this book with others.

Wonderful as:

★ *An inspiration to any parent*

★ *Use as part of a parenting class curriculum*

★ *Youth group gift to parents of teenagers*

★ *An encouragement to family members*

Multiple copies as low as $7 each! **_(See page 112.)_**

DON'T JUST PROTECT YOUR CHILDREN'S BODIES: PROTECT TRUTH THEIR MINDS AS WELL.

Over 70% of churched youth walk away from their faith in college.

WHY?

Because they have not connected the Bible to the physical world around them, nor do they know the evidence which shows the Bible to be the most credible book on Earth.

This 144 page book is the result of a 12-year effort to bring the scientific evidence for creation into public view. *Search for the Truth* documents the firestorm that results when the evidence for creation is placed in public newspapers. Permission is granted to use the 83 extensively illustrated, one-page articles in your local paper or church newsletter. *Search for the Truth* is just plain fun to read.

A one-of-a-kind daily devotional harmonizing science to Biblical teaching, This 408 page book starts each day with yet another reason to trust God's word. It is organized into 26 different subject areas and draws from over 50 expert sources. These "creation sound bites" give 365 awe-inspiring examples of God's incredible workmanship.

America has more Bible colleges; seminaries; church denominations; Christian books; tapes and videos; evangelistic outreaches; Christian bookstores; and Christian radio stations than any other country on earth. Yet, we are on the verge of legitimizing homosexual "marriage," we cannot mention Jesus in public schools, and every reminder of our Christian foundation is systematically being removed from public view. This 128-page book is the perfect resource for those who do not understand why we are losing our Christian heritage.

See these resources at www.searchforthetruth.net or order on page 112.

To order *Search for the Truth* resources, send a check and this order form to:

Search for the Truth
3275 E. Monroe Road
Midland, MI 48642
989-837-5546

Order online at www.SEARCHFORTHETRUTH.net

MIX & MATCH
all books for the lowest cost:
1 copy @ $12.95
10 or more copies @ $7.00 each

Shipping charges:
1- 9 books = $2 per book
10 or more books - $1 per book
Please call for case pricing.

ITEM	QUANTITY	COST EA.	TOTAL
Protecting His Workmanship			
A Closer Look at the Evidence			
Search for the Truth			
By His Word			
		SUBTOTAL	
		MI RESIDENTS ADD 6% SALES TAX	
		SHIPPING (see above for charges)	
		TOTAL	

ship to:

Name: ______________________

Address: ______________________

City/State/ZIP: ______________________

Phone: ______________ **e-mail:** ______________

THANK YOU